Strange

Things

in silence

Cathy mazie carnation

TABLE OF CONTENTS

CHAPTER 1 Where the Light Lives 1

CHAPTER 2 When the Darkness Tried to Kill Me 6

CHAPTER 3 Living on a Highway for the Dead 13

CHAPTER 4 The Day Heaven Sent Me Back..............................21

CHAPTER 5 Two Worlds Under One Roof 30

CHAPTER 6 Learning Not to Fear What I Can See......................38

CHAPTER 7 Protecting My Peace Above All Else 47

CHAPTER 8 What the Light Teaches in the Dark.........................55

CHAPTER 9 Breaking the Silence for Those Like Me 67

CHAPTER 10 The Woman Darkness Cannot Silence....................77

CHAPTER 1
WHERE THE LIGHT LIVES

The ocean has always been my sanctuary. It's not just a place for me; it's a feeling, a rhythm, a breath. From the moment I arrive, whether the sun is blazing overhead, casting diamonds across the waves, or the moon is high, painting silver ripples that shimmer like whispered secrets, the sea offers a serenity that wraps around me like a warm, fuzzy blanket. As the day unfolds, even in the hazy blue of early evening, when the horizon blurs and the world seems to exhale, everything slows.

At the beach, my mind quiets. My heart steadies. I breathe differently, deeper, fuller, as if every inhale is rinsing away something heavy I've carried for far too long. Something I don't always name. Something that clings to me in places where the air doesn't move, and the shadows stretch too long.

It doesn't matter if the sand is crowded with families and laughter or if I'm the only soul for miles. The peace I find there isn't dictated by silence or solitude; it's something internal, something unlocked only when I'm standing barefoot with my toes buried in warm grains of sand, and the ocean stretching endlessly ahead like a promise. Once I settle in, I can read for hours, let music wash over me, or simply close my eyes and drift into dreams. And yes, I'll admit it: there's a quiet joy in coming home with a golden tan that glows through the winter months. It's more than just sun-kissed skin; it's a soft, glowing reminder of time well spent, of laughter carried on sea breezes and afternoons that stretched lazily into twilight.

Over the years, I've wandered many shores: Jersey, Myrtle Beach, Florida, and each one has offered that same refuge. The scenery shifts, the accents change, the boardwalks vary in charm, but the feeling remains constant. It's as if the ocean speaks a language only I understand, one that transcends geography and time. In Jersey, I remember the scent of salt and funnel cakes mingling in the air, the sound of seagulls squabbling over dropped fries, and the way the boardwalk lights flickered like stars as night fell. Myrtle Beach had its own magic: long stretches of soft sand, the hum of live music drifting from beach bars, and the thrill of spotting dolphins just beyond the breakers. Florida was warmth incarnate: palm trees swaying, the sun so strong it felt like a hug, and water so clear it seemed unreal.

Each beach I've visited has its own distinct personality, shaped not just by its landscape but by the memories I've made there. Jersey is nostalgic, a place of childhood memories and teenage summers. Myrtle Beach is lively, full of color and movement, where the days stretch long and the nights are filled with laughter. Florida, by contrast, is tranquil and meditative with pastel sunsets and gentle tides. But despite their differences, they all offer me the same thing: peace. A kind of peace I've never been able to replicate anywhere else.

Perhaps it's because I'm never truly alone there. My best friend and sister-in-law, Dottie, is often by my side. She's the kind of person who listens without judgment, who laughs with me in joy and sits with me in sorrow. Our thirty-year friendship is stitched together with honesty, shared secrets, and a daily 6:30 p.m. phone call; a ritual so steady it has become the heartbeat of my days. We've walked countless beaches together, collecting shells, sharing stories, and sometimes just sitting in silence, letting the waves speak for us. I remember one evening in Myrtle Beach when we watched the sun dip below the horizon, our feet in the surf, and Dottie turned to me and said, "This is what peace feels like." She was right.

We've had our share of adventures, getting caught in sudden downpours, losing flip-flops to the tide, and laughing until our stomachs hurt over inside jokes that no one else would understand. But more than anything, we've shared the quiet moments. The ones where the world fades away, and it's just us, the ocean, and the comfort of knowing we're safe. There's something sacred about those moments. They're the ones I carry with me when life gets hard.

But the beach offers more than just companionship and calm; it offers refuge. A kind of spiritual stillness I can't seem to find anywhere else. Because spirits don't follow me there.

At home, I live with uninvited spiritual disturbances: whispers in the dark, shadows that linger too long, a presence that chills the air. It's a reality I've learned to navigate, but never fully escaped from. There are nights when I wake up to the sound of footsteps in an empty hallway, or feel a cold breath on my neck with no one nearby. I've seen lights flicker, doors creak open on their own, and once, a mirror cracked without reason. My house, though filled with love and memories, has corners that feel heavy, and rooms that seem to hold their breath. There are places in my home I avoid after dark, not because of superstition, but because of experience. I've learned to keep certain doors closed, to sleep with a light on, to ignore the occasional whisper that doesn't belong to anyone living.

Yet at the shore, I am untouched. I've never seen a paranormal investigation unfold on the sand, never felt the weight of something unseen pressing against my peace. Maybe it's the heat; spirits, from my experience, seem to prefer the cold. Or maybe it's the distractions:

the rhythmic crash of waves, the golden light, the laughter of strangers, the pages of a book flipping in the breeze. Whatever the reason, the beach is a place where the darkness cannot reach me. And that safety is priceless.

Strangely enough, I love reading horror novels by the water. Stephen King is my favorite. His stories don't scare me; how could they, when my own life has been haunted in ways his characters will never quite know? Fictional fear feels harmless in comparison. The monsters in those books stay in their pages, but the ones I face don't. But at the beach, even those stories feel lighter. I can read about haunted houses and cursed towns while the sun warms my skin and the ocean hums its lullaby. It's a beautiful contradiction: dark tales in a place of light.

I remember one afternoon in Florida, stretched out on a towel with Pet Sematary in my hands and the waves crashing just feet away. The story was chilling, but the sun was so bright, and the air so warm that I felt invincible. That moment stayed with me, not because of the fear in the pages, but because of the peace around me. It reminded me that fear doesn't have to consume us. We can face darkness and still choose light.

That contrast is what makes the beach feel sacred. The beach is an open place, free from walls, closets, and shadows. At home, spiritual activity creeps into corners and catches me alone. But at the shore, the openness swallows any darkness. I can sip coffee on the boardwalk at sunrise, stroll with the waves licking at my ankles, or simply sit in a chair and lose myself in a story. There's no need to look over my shoulder. No need to brace for the chill. Just me, the sea, and the quiet joy of being present.

That sense of peace is more than a temporary escape; it's a longing. If I could, I'd live there full-time. Maybe not right on the ocean, but close enough to hear the waves at night, to let their rhythm lull me to sleep. Life, finances, and obligations make that dream complicated, but the pull is always there. I know one day I'll find my way. The ocean calls to me, and I believe it will welcome me home when the time is right.

I've looked at beachside rentals, imagined what it would be like to wake up to the sound of gulls and the scent of salt. I've pictured a small cottage with wide windows, a porch swing, and a path that leads straight to the sand. I'd fill it with books, seashells, and laughter. Dottie would have her own room, of course, and we'd spend our days exploring, reading, and simply being. It's a dream, yes, but one that feels possible. One that feels necessary.

When I think back to the first time I felt that peace, the moment the shore whispered safety into my bones, I wish I could reach out to that version of myself. I'd tell her, *You've found your safe place. Never let it go.* Because that's what the beach gives me. Not just escape but renewal. Not just quiet, but joy. It's a reminder that life can still be light. That healing is possible. That peace isn't a myth, but a place you can stand in, barefoot and free.

And maybe that's the truth I've been chasing all along: no matter how heavy life becomes, there's a place where breath returns, where shadows lift, and where the soul remembers how to rest. For me, that place will always be the beach.

CHAPTER 2
WHEN THE DARKNESS
TRIED TO KILL ME

Every house has a room you don't like. Some rooms you love, places that feel like they remember you, like they're glad you came back. Others you pass through without thinking, just like a part of the route from fridge to couch or bed to bathroom. And then there's the one. The room that never feels right, no matter what you do. You paint it, rearrange it, open the windows, light a candle, but it doesn't matter. It stays wrong regardless. In our house, that room was the drum room.

It sat at the end of the hallway like it was waiting for something. Not someone—something. I never liked going in there. It was always too cool, too dark, too still. Even in summer, when the rest of the house felt like it was sweating, the drum room stayed cold. The light barely reached. I can't explain it better than that—it just felt wrong. If you've ever walked into a place and instantly thought *Nope*, that's exactly it. That's how it was for me. Every time.

Bob never noticed. He could sit in there for hours, drumming with his headphones on, lost in the rhythm, completely at ease. To him, it was his creative space, his zone. He'd talk about the acoustics, the way the sound bounced just right off the walls. He loved that room. I didn't. To me, it was a place I avoided unless I had no choice. I'd walk past it quickly, eyes forward, like I could escape the feeling it gave me.

That day started out so normal. I was off from work, curled up in my favorite chair, half-watching some movie I'd seen a dozen times. Sunlight came through the curtains in streaks, and the air conditioner hummed like it always did. It felt calm, safe. Ordinary. The kind of day that makes you forget the weird corners of your house.

Then the phone rang.

It was Bob. His voice was casual, like he was reminding me to grab milk on the way home. "Don't forget, your telescope lenses are up in the drum room on the table."

Just like that, the calm cracked. The telescope had been my birthday gift. He'd spent hours putting it together in secret, making sure everything was adjusted perfectly, just so he could surprise me. That's Bob—when he wants to, he can be thoughtful like that. The telescope itself wasn't the problem. It was beautiful, actually. Sleek, silver, full of promise. I'd been excited to use it, to point it at the sky and feel small in a good way. But where did he leave the lenses? That was the problem—up in the damn drum room.

He could've left them anywhere, on the kitchen counter, by the bookshelf, even on the floor next to the telescope itself. Hell, I would've taken the bathroom sink. But no. He chose the one place in the house I hated. The one room that made my skin crawl. The one space that felt like it didn't want me in it.

I didn't say anything on the phone. Just made a sound that passed for agreement and hung up. Then I sat there for a very long time. Not doing anything, just staring at the hallway like it might blink first. Debating. *Do I really want to go up there? I could wait until he came home and make him grab them. He wouldn't mind. But he'd laugh.*

He'd tease me, call me dramatic, scared for nothing. And I'd have to pretend it didn't bother me. Do I want to deal with that? Not really.

I kept thinking, *if I'd just gone already, I'd be back by now.* That kind of logic—the kind that pushes you into things you don't want to do. It's the voice that nudges you toward things you'd rather avoid, whispering that hesitation is weakness. So finally, I sighed and pushed myself out of the chair. My legs felt heavier than they should've been, like my body knew where I was headed and wasn't thrilled about it.

At the top of the stairs, I stopped. The hallway was bright, daylight spilling in, warm and normal. The kind of light that usually made the house feel safe. But something was off. The air shifted. Heavier. The hum of the air conditioner, usually background noise, felt louder now, pressing out through the closed drum room door like a warning.

I stared at the door.

It looked the same as always. White paint, slightly chipped near the handle. But the light didn't want to go past it. It stopped just short, like it had drawn a line. Like even the hallway was saying, *Don't do it.*

But I did it anyway. I opened the door.

The second I stepped inside, the air hit me. Cold, heavy, thick. Almost vibrating. It clung to my skin like a damp cloth, vibrating faintly as if the room itself was humming. Goosebumps rose instantly on my arms. Not from the temperature alone—something else. Something deeper. There was no smell. No dust, no metal, no mildew. Just stillness. A suffocating silence that felt intentional. Like the room had been waiting. Like it had noticed me.

I thought about pulling the chain for the ceiling light. The string dangled just above my head, swaying slightly, like it was daring me.

But I didn't bother with the light. I didn't need it. The layout of the room was etched into my memory—every corner, every shadow. I knew exactly where the table was. And if I'm being honest, I already knew I wasn't alone.

That's how it always felt in there. Watched.

Not the kind of watching you can brush off. Not the vague paranoia of an overactive imagination. This was different. This was targeted. Intentional. Like something in the room had eyes, and they were fixed on me the moment I crossed the threshold. But no. I wasn't staying in there one second longer than I had to. I could see the table. I knew exactly where the lenses were. No need to linger. So I crossed the room in a blur, snatched the lenses off the table like they might burn me, and turned around, and in that moment, I knew. Someone was right behind me. Not a sound. Not a breath. But the air shifted. The kind of shift you feel in your bones before your brain catches up. My skin went tight. My stomach dropped. Every instinct screamed *move. Get out!* I bolted.

I ran straight out and slammed the door shut behind me with a force that rattled the frame. The sound echoed down the hallway: sharp, final, like a gunshot. I thought I was safe. I really did.

That's when it happened. No warning. No sound. Just violence. Out of nowhere, something grabbed me by the throat.

One second, I was moving, the next, I wasn't. I was yanked off my feet like a rag doll and slammed against the hallway wall so hard I saw stars. My back hit with a crack, and the breath was knocked clean out of me. My feet dangled, kicking uselessly against the air. I couldn't breathe. I couldn't scream. The grip around my neck was like ice-cold, merciless fingers long and strong, wrapped all the way around, choking the life out of me.

The force was monstrous, inhuman. Not just strong—*wrong*. Like it didn't belong in this world. Like it had never been human to begin with. In that instant, I knew, this thing didn't want to scare me. It didn't want to warn me. It wanted me gone. Dead.

Panic detonated inside me. My chest burned, lungs screaming for air that wouldn't come. My throat was closing, crushed under fingers that felt like iron dipped in ice. My brain scrambled for logic, for reason, for anything that could explain this. *Was I dreaming? Hallucinating? Had I finally lost my grip?* But no. The pain was real. The pressure was real. The choking was real. My body was failing. My vision blurred at the edges. My limbs were useless, flailing against something that didn't yield.

For a second, I thought, *This is it.* This is how I go. But then something else surged up from the pit of me. Defiance. A raw, primal refusal. A voice inside of me that roared louder than the fear: *No.* You are not taking me out like this. Not here. Not now. Not like this.

I couldn't fight it with my hands; it wasn't solid. It was shadow and hatred and something older than language. And my only weapon was faith. So I reached for it. I wasn't silent.

Inside, I was screaming. Not with my voice, my throat was locked tight, but with everything else. My mind, my heart, my spirit. I threw it out over and over, like flares into the dark: *Help me. Help me. Archangel Michael, God please, God please!* I begged. I pleaded. I demanded. The words tumbled out in a rush, tangled and raw, each one a desperate gasp, each one a final plea. I didn't care how it sounded. I didn't care if it made sense. I just needed *someone* to hear me.

And then… they came. A rush. A sweep sound, sharp and final, like the air itself had been cut open. The grip vanished. I dropped hard to the floor, knees cracking against the wood, clutching the lenses tight in my hand like a talisman. Not because I needed them, but because I needed something to hold onto. Something real. Something mine.

I gasped for air, lungs clawing at the silence. My chest burned like fire had bloomed inside it. My throat ached, raw and bruised, each breath scraping through like broken glass. My body trembled so violently I could barely stay upright. My limbs felt like paper: thin, fragile, barely there. My skin buzzed with leftover terror, like the fear hadn't left, just settled deeper. But I was alive. Archangel Michael had come. God had answered.

I lay there, curled around the pain and the relief, trying to breathe, trying to remember how to be in my body again. The silence was deafening. The absence of that thing was louder than its presence had been.

When I finally moved, I crawled to the banister, gripped it with both hands, and went down the stairs slow. One step at a time. Whispering thank you with every footfall. By the time I reached the bottom, my legs barely worked. My body felt like it had been hollowed out and filled with static. I was still shaky, but alive. Safe.

Bob? He believed me when I told him. He didn't laugh. He just shrugged and said, "Well, they don't bother me." That's Bob. He doesn't want to talk about it because it scares him. He'll never admit it outright, but I see it, the way he stiffens when the room goes quiet. The way he pauses when he smells cigarette smoke out of nowhere.

No one's smoking. No one's even been here. But he smells it. That's as far as he'll go. He knows something's there—he just doesn't want to face it. But I know what I felt. I know what tried to take me. And I know what saved me.

That day taught me something I'll carry forever: fear feeds them. That's what they want. That's what they thrive on. If you give in, they win. But if you fight, if you call on the light, they can't hold you. They can't stay. It's not about being fearless. It's about refusing to surrender.

I'll never forget that.

CHAPTER 3
LIVING ON A HIGHWAY
FOR THE DEAD

When Bob and I moved into Levittown in 1997, it felt like we were stepping into a brand-new life. Not just a new chapter, but a whole new book. We were young, hopeful, and ready to build something of our own. The very first time we saw the house, it wasn't empty. A family still lived there—kids darting from room to room, toys scattered across the floor like confetti after a party, the air thick with the kind of noise only laughter and sibling squabbles can create. It was chaotic, yes, but it was the kind of chaos that made the house feel alive. I wasn't thinking about ghosts or history or who had lived there before. I wasn't wondering about the stories the walls might hold. All I could think was, *I want this house.* It was bigger than anything I'd had before, a single home just for us, and the moment I walked through the door, I knew. It was mine. And I was going to get it.

From the outside, it looked so ordinary. Nothing flashy, nothing that screamed for attention. Gray shingles blanketed the roof, black trim framed the windows, and a solid black front door stood like a quiet sentinel. The wide living room window spilled daylight onto the street, casting long shadows in the afternoon sun. A gentle slope of grass rolled down from the front steps to a driveway lined with trees that whispered in the breeze. There was no garage. What had once been one had been transformed into a dining room with a big window that caught the morning light just right.

Inside, the layout was simple, almost intuitive. You walked in, and the stairs rose right in front of you, leading to the bedrooms above. To the left, the living room stretched out, open and inviting, flowing seamlessly into the dining area. Beyond that, a laundry room tucked itself neatly into the corner, and the kitchen, bright and functional, sat at the back with sliding glass doors that opened to a backyard full of grass, flowers, and possibility. It was neat. It was suburban. It was perfect.

At least, it looked that way.

On moving day, with boxes in my arms, sweat sticking to my back, and a hundred things on my mind. I stepped through the front door and froze. Three ghosts were sitting calmly on the steps, like they'd been waiting for me. Not faint outlines, not tricks of the light: three clear figures, watching. My stomach dropped. My mind didn't even try to make sense of it. It just shouted: *You have got to be kidding me.* I set the box down slowly, careful not to make a sound, turned right back around, and walked outside as if my leaving would somehow reset what I'd seen. Like maybe I'd imagined it. I stood there for a minute, staring at the trees, the sky, the driveway, anything but the house. Then I went back in. They were gone. But it was too late. The house had already revealed itself. And I knew, deep down, I was in trouble.

The house sits on a hill, and just two hundred feet down the road, past a stand of trees that always look darker than they should at night, a creek cuts across the land. A small wooden bridge spans it, just wide enough to walk across. In daylight, it looks harmless; quaint, even. But after a storm, it swells, rushing loud, the water tugging at the roots along its banks. After a storm, it swells and roars, tugging at the roots along its banks like it's trying to pull the earth apart. The water rushes with a kind of fury that feels unnatural, like it's angry at something it can't name. And at night, that little bridge becomes eerie—like it's waiting for something. The creek isn't just water, it's a pull. Something deep and steady, like its calling to whatever still lingers nearby. I didn't notice it all at once. It crept in slowly, like a fog rolling in under the door. At first, it was just a feeling. I'd be sitting in the living room at night, pretending to relax with the TV on, and I'd feel it—movement. Not inside the house exactly, but through it. Like a breeze that didn't come from any window. A presence that didn't belong to me. I'd see spirits, gliding past me, walking down toward the creek and back again, as if my house sits directly on their path.

They'd glide silently through walls and doorways, shadows slipping across the corner of my eye. Sometimes one at a time, sometimes two or three together. Sometimes a whole current of them, like a tide moving through the rooms. The air drops cold when they pass, heavy enough to press into my skin like a damp cloth.

It wasn't just the chill that unsettled me. It was the moments when their presence became undeniable. Once, brushing my hair in the bedroom mirror, I saw a man crawl straight out of the wall behind me. His head was bowed, his clothes streaked with dirt, his whole body sunk into a tired slump. He never looked at me. He just trudged forward, crossed the room, and went straight into the opposite wall. He didn't see me; he didn't care I was there. I stood frozen, comb in my hand, pity curling in my stomach. That poor soul was locked into his loop forever, and I knew it wasn't the last time I'd see him.

Most of them don't make noise. They move in silence, caught in whatever dream-state holds them. But when they want my attention, they let me know. A shuffle on the floorboards. A knock. The kind of sound that makes you whisper, *What was that?* And if you dare to ask them to do it again, they do. That's how I know.

Curiosity, of course, is a dangerous thing. I didn't want to open the door any wider, but it claws at you. And my friend? She leaned into it like it was a calling. She had the gear, the obsession, the habit of walking into places that felt wrong to everyone else. Empty houses, abandoned buildings, graveyards after dark. She carried her EVP recorder and spirit box like other people carried flashlights, always listening, always waiting for the faintest trace of a voice.

One evening, she looked around my living room with the same spark she had when she'd tell me about some old farmhouse or a deserted school she'd prowled through. "You know," she said, "we don't have to go anywhere else. Let's set it up here."

And so we did. We set the recorders in the living room, sometimes in my bedroom. The air always felt wrong before we even started— cooler, heavier, like the house knew what we were about to invite. My shepherds would pad in, rigid with unease, pressing themselves against me like living shields made of fur and fear.

"Ask," my friend would whisper.

So I did. My voice barely made it past my lips. "Is anyone here?"

At first, just static. Then, cutting through it: *"Joe."*

I jumped, my water glass nearly slipping from my hand. My mouth went dry. "What's your name?" I asked.

The box crackled, spat, and answered sharp: *"Harry."*

The air dropped colder. Goosebumps lifted across my arms. My shepherds growled low, eyes fixed on the corner of the room. Then a third voice pushed through, louder than the rest: *"Michael."*

Always first names. Mostly men. Never the year they died. Ask them, and they don't remember. Sometimes they don't even seem to remember who they were. Too many years passed, too many lifetimes lost. But names they can give, snapped out of the air like a claim.

And if you ask them to come closer, they do. Because they're drawn to me, people say it's my glow. Everyone has one, but mine is gold, and they see it. They know I'll hear. They know I'll help. But when they come close, they drain me. My chest feels heavy, my body suddenly tired, like they're feeding off the energy that keeps me upright. That's the price of opening. And once you've opened the door, you don't get to choose who walks through.

Even my son felt it. Mike would lie in his room upstairs and tell me he knew something was there, but he shut it out. "I don't want to be like you, Mom," he said. "I don't want them." And he was right. Some people close themselves off, seal the cracks, and it never touches them. But I can't. My door is open whether I want it or not.

Sometimes the spirits come as more than shadows. Once, I saw my sister-in-law Linda, younger than I'd ever known her. She walked toward me in jeans and a plaid shirt, her hair shining, her face soft and healthy. She had died in a nursing home, sick and aged. I hadn't even known she had passed when I saw her. She smiled from the other side and said, *Kat, I'm so sorry for how I treated you.* She had been cruel in life. Cold and dismissive. And I hadn't forgiven her. But in that moment, I saw the truth: even death couldn't hide her shame. She came because she knew I would see her. Because she knew I would listen.

The dead come because they know I will see them.

For me, nights are hardest. I try to sleep, but it comes broken, in jolts and gasps. Awake at one, then three, until by four I give up. Sometimes I feel a hand on my shoulder, cold and urgent, trying to wake me up from a dream I didn't even know I was in. Sometimes shadows glide past the foot of my bed and vanish into the wall like they were never there.

I don't leave the bedroom at night. If I have to pee, forget it. I hold it till the next morning.

My shepherds lie on the floor like stone, eyes tracking things I can't always see, a low growl building in their chests. They are my protectors, but even they can't keep the cold spots away. Step into the wrong place, and it's like walking into an invisible freezer. Sometimes there's pressure on my chest, so heavy I whisper, "All right— whatever you need, I'll hear you."

There's no scent to them. Not flowers, not perfume, not rot. Just the clean, hard absence of anything living. It's not what they bring, it's what they take. The warmth. The stillness. The sense of being alone.

I've tried crucifixes, candles, and holy water. They're here anyway. This isn't Dracula. Faith helps me, yes! It gives me armor, strength, the light I call on when I need it, but objects alone won't stop the current. The house doesn't care what I hang on the walls. When guests come, I shut myself down so they don't notice. I want them to be comfortable. I don't need anyone bolting out the door. But most people, even family, don't have the ability to sense it anyway. They walk through the rooms like it's just a house. But it's not. Bob, for example, refuses to acknowledge it.

He hides upstairs in his drum room, safe in rhythm and denial. He says they don't bother him, and they don't. He has no ability, no glow. Spirits ignore him. But I was a threat to the evil one upstairs, and it attacked me for that reason alone. Because I knew Bob wouldn't talk about it. He doesn't want to know. And I don't push. Some people are better off not knowing.

Still, the house doesn't stay quiet for long. Once, a TV paranormal crew camped outside our house for a whole weekend. Tall poles rose into the sky, cameras and lights pointed down at our roof like we were a crime scene. Neighbors gathered, whispering, pointing. After that, letters started coming. People all over Levittown saying, *We have activity, too.*

It made sense. This land used to be fields, settled centuries ago. People died here and were buried wherever they fell. I'm not the only one who sees. But I am the one who carries the gold glow, and that makes me the one they seek.

Do I feel cursed? No. I feel lucky. Chosen. A woman once told me that when I was two and nearly died, I sat on Jesus' lap and He sent me back with a gift. Maybe this is it. Maybe this is my job. When spirits linger, I open the light and point the way. *There. Go there. That's where your family is. That's where peace waits.* And some of them go. Not all. But enough.

Still, the gift costs. It costs me my sleep, it costs me my silence, it costs me the chance to ever live an ordinary life. That's why I love the beach. The Jersey shore, Myrtle Beach, Florida. Give me a chair, an umbrella, ice-cold water, and Dottie by my side with a book, and I can finally breathe. The waves hush the whispers. The spirits don't follow me there. The sun presses warm on my skin, and for once, I can lose myself in a scary story, knowing the fear on the page isn't mine.

But the beach always ends. And when I come home, it's back to the hill, back to the creek, back to the little bridge waiting at night like a mouth. Back to the house that looks like every other house on the street, but isn't. My house is on a road. A highway for the dead. And every night, as footsteps brush past my door, I remind myself: this is my gift. This is my burden. This is my home.

CHAPTER 4
THE DAY HEAVEN
SENT ME BACK

I was only two years old when it happened, but the story has stayed with me for as long as I can remember. Most of what I know about that day came later, through my mother's trembling voice as she tried to explain what she saw. It was August 22, a hot and bright summer afternoon. The sun hung lazily in the sky, casting long shadows across the porch, and everything felt still, as if the world itself had paused to breathe. I was sitting on the top step of our porch beside my brother, Walt, our legs dangling, our fingers sticky from popsicles. My mother rested nearby in her chair, watching us play with the quiet contentment of someone who believed the day held no surprises. There was nothing unusual about that day. No tension in the air, no sign of what was coming. Just the hum of summer, cicadas buzzing, a lawn mower droning in the distance, the occasional bark of a dog.

Somewhere beyond our quiet street, another family was laughing, celebrating a birthday with balloons and cake. I didn't know it then, but that same day, far from our porch, another child's life was beginning to intertwine with mine in a way neither of us could have imagined.

And then, in a single breath, everything changed.

No one heard a gunshot. Not my mother, not the neighbors, not a single soul. Years later, she would tell me how it happened, how one moment I was upright, giggling at something Walt had said, and the next, I was falling backward. My head struck the cement with a sickening thud. Blood poured down my face, fast and heavy, painting the steps in crimson. She screamed for my father, grabbed the nearest towel, anything she could find, to stop the bleeding. Her hands trembled as she pressed the fabric to my head, her eyes wide with disbelief. People came running from their homes, drawn by her panic. The street, moments ago so quiet, filled with voices—frantic, confused, and desperate to understand. But no one knew what had happened. There had been no warning, no sound, no visible threat. Just a child, suddenly bleeding, and a mother trying to hold her world together.

Someone had fired a gun; that much was clear, but no one saw who it was or where it came from. Police flooded the street, searching rooftops and yards, combing through hedges and alleyways. Eventually, they found shell casings across the street. They decided someone had fired a gun recklessly, and the bullet had ricocheted, striking me by chance. A freak accident, they called it. A tragic anomaly. But even as I grew older, even as the story was retold with the same sterile phrasing, I never believed it was just an accident.

My parents rushed me to the hospital, desperate for help. The first hospital turned us away. The wound was too severe, they said. My mother begged, her voice cracking with fear, but the answer remained the same. There was nothing they could do. So my father drove on, gripping the wheel with white knuckles, praying aloud as he sped through traffic. My mother held me close, pressing the towel to my head, whispering promises she wasn't sure she could keep. The chaos blurred. Sirens faded. Voices dissolved into a distant hum. And then, there was silence.

I wasn't in pain anymore. I wasn't even there.

I was somewhere else entirely.

I remember sitting on someone's lap, surrounded by warmth and peace. The air felt soft, like a blanket woven from light. It felt safe, like nothing could ever hurt me again. Even as a little girl, I knew who it was. I didn't need to be told. Jesus sat in a high-backed chair, and I was curled up on His lap. The love I felt in that moment was unlike anything I'd ever known. It wasn't just comforting, but it was complete. His voice was gentle yet filled every part of me, like music that had always been playing in the background of my soul. He looked at me with infinite tenderness and said, *"Little one, it's not your time. I'm sending you back with a gift."*

His voice carried love instead of fear. I cried, clinging to the warmth of that place, begging to stay. But in the blink of an eye, everything changed.

Suddenly, I was back.

My mother's face hovered above me, her eyes wide with panic. The hospital lights were blinding, voices were shouting over one another, and the world rushed in all at once.

Later, the doctors explained what had happened. They told me the bullet had entered just beneath my scalp, right in the center of my head. Miraculously, it hadn't penetrated deeper. The doctors removed it, leaving only a small scar, a tiny mark that holds more memory than any photograph ever could. After the hospital, the story faded into silence. No one in my family spoke of it again. There were no newspaper clippings on the fridge, no framed headlines, no whispered acknowledgments over dinner. My parents carried a haunted silence, as if by never mentioning it they could make it disappear. But I remembered. I always did.

As a child, I only knew what my mother told me: that I had fallen, that I had been hurt, and that somehow, I had survived. Her version was simple, almost soothing in its vagueness. But deep inside, I carried another memory, one I could never explain. A light. A voice. A peace that never truly left me. It lived quietly within me, like a secret I didn't yet have words to share.

For years, that was enough. I accepted the story I'd been given, even as something deeper stirred beneath it. Then, one afternoon, long after the incident had faded from everyday conversation, a neighbor told me she recalled that day differently, that my mother had walked up the street to talk with friends, leaving Walt and me on the porch alone. When the bullet struck, Walt had tried to pull me up the street to find her, both of us covered in blood. Her version of events unsettled me. It didn't match the story I'd always known. Maybe she was right; maybe not. Pain reshapes memory. Still, hearing her words reminded me it had all been real, that it wasn't just a story I'd imagined into being.

For a long time, I didn't know what to believe. My mother's story was all I had, until I began to search for the truth myself. Much later, I found the old newspaper articles buried in the archives. Just a few short lines about a little girl struck by a stray bullet. Just a brief mention, printed and forgotten. But holding those yellowed pages made everything real again. The world had called it an accident; the papers had moved on, and the neighbors had long forgotten. But I hadn't. For me, each scrap of proof deepened the mystery. It confirmed what my family had endured, but it didn't explain what I had seen. That was a truth only heaven could answer. And that was when I began to sense that what happened wasn't only survival. It was an awakening.

As I grew older, I began to understand that gifts from heaven aren't always easy to bear. The gift He gave me as a child was one of the hardest things you could ever give to a little girl. Seeing what others could not was both a blessing and a burden. At night, I would see spirits, some gentle, some lost, moving quietly through my room. Sometimes they stood beside my bed; sometimes they sat and waited, not realizing they were gone. I never knew what they wanted, only that they were there. In those moments, a woman would appear. She wasn't like the others. She glowed with a calm that stilled the air around her. An angel, really. She would place her finger to her lips and whisper, "Don't react. Don't cry. If you do, people will think you're crazy, and they'll send you away."

So I learned silence. Even at school, I learned to keep my eyes down. If I stared too long at something others couldn't see, they'd whisper or laugh. So I pretended not to notice. I learned to keep my eyes open and my voice still. I became a quiet observer in a world that didn't know I was watching more than they could see.

Not long after I came home from the hospital, the visions began, figures drifting through rooms, their eyes filled with confusion and longing. It was as if the doorway between life and death had never quite closed. I would lie in bed and feel the air shift, the quiet fill with unseen presence. That was when the woman came most often, the same one who had taught me to stay still. She would appear in the hush of the night to remind me that not all who wander are meant to frighten. "Don't be afraid," she would whisper. "You've been chosen to help."

Her words became a thread I held onto as I grew. I knew I was different, but I also knew my gift came from God. I saw the good and the bad, the light and the dark. I saw souls who were lost and helped them find peace. It frightened me at times, yes, but even in the fear, I felt honored. I understood that He had trusted me with this for a reason. Even with all the fear and confusion, I felt honored that He had trusted me with this for a reason.

Years passed, and the gift remained, quiet but constant. Then, in my thirties, something happened that changed everything. My daughter was planning her wedding and visited an old chapel. While there, she met a woman who asked to see me. I didn't know her, had never met her. My daughter said, "Mom, there's someone at the chapel who wants to meet you." "Who?" I asked, surprised.

"I don't know," she said, "but she asked for you by name."

I remember feeling uneasy as I walked into that chapel. The air was thick with age, and the light filtering through stained glass painted the room in muted colors. Dust floated in the beams like tiny spirits. The woman greeted me at the door with a kind smile and gestured for me to sit down on an old velvet sofa near the altar. I still remember how my hands felt cold against the fabric, how the silence in that room seemed to hold its breath.

And then she said the words that froze me.

"You were the little girl who sat on His lap."

I stared at her, certain I had misheard. "I'm sorry?" I said. "What did you just say?"

"You were the child," she repeated softly. "The one who sat on His lap. You saw Him when you were hurt."

My heart stopped. I felt the air leave my lungs. I hadn't told anyone, not my parents, not my friends, not even my husband. How could she possibly know?

She continued, describing it all in exact detail: the high-backed chair, the light that surrounded Him, the feeling of peace that wrapped around me like a blanket. And then, she repeated His words… the very ones I had carried in silence for decades: 'Little one, it's not your time. I'm sending you back with a gift.'

I sat frozen, every breath shallow. "You don't know me," I whispered. "You can't know that."

But she only smiled gently, her eyes steady and kind. "He wanted me to tell you that your gift was real, that it came from Him. He sent you back for a reason."

For a moment, I thought I might faint. My daughter hadn't told this woman anything. She didn't even share my last name; there was no way for her to have found me or to have known those sacred details. I remember leaving that chapel, trembling, my whole body weak, my heart pounding like a drum. I didn't speak for a long time on the drive home. The silence between my daughter and me was filled with something larger than words, something holy. It was as though heaven itself had reached through time to remind me that what began in pain still had purpose.

That meeting left me shaken to my core. It was no longer a story or a fading childhood memory; it was a truth affirmed by someone who couldn't possibly have known. And soon after, I learned that the same hand that sent me back had already begun weaving my life into Bob's.

In that moment, everything I had carried silently for years found its voice. What I had seen as a child, what I had tried for so long to convince myself was only a dream, was suddenly confirmed. The woman in the chapel didn't tell me the story for the first time; she revealed that heaven had never forgotten it.

I left that chapel trembling, my body weak, my heart pounding with something more than fear. And not long after, I learned just how far that purpose had stretched.

Many years later, long after Bob and I were married, I discovered the full truth about that day. The day I was shot, the day my life should have ended, was the same day Bob turned ten. While I was being carried to the hospital, unconscious and bleeding, he was blowing out candles and laughing with his family. Two children, living two very different moments, bound by something unseen. Maybe it was a coincidence. Maybe it was divine alignment. But I believe it was God's way of tying our stories together long before we met. The day I nearly died was the day my future was being prepared. It was as if the universe had whispered, "Not yet. There's more to come."

Even now, I think about how one heartbeat can split a life into "before" and "after." That single moment, so quiet, so sudden, became the hinge on which everything turned. Maybe that's why I still wonder what I would ask Him if I could sit on His lap again. I think I'd ask, *"Why are there bad people in the world?"* Not out of anger, but out of longing to understand the pain we carry.

But perhaps we aren't meant to know all the answers. Maybe faith isn't in the knowing, but in trusting that every question, every ache, every mystery draws us closer to light. Maybe the gift isn't clarity, but the courage to walk forward without it.

When I look back now, I don't see blood or fear or pain. I see His face. I feel the warmth that wraps around me like a promise. I remember His voice saying, *"It's not your time."* And I know He was right. Because that was the day everything began, the day I received my gift, the day Bob celebrated his, and the day our two stories quietly became one.

And as the years unfolded, that truth only deepened. What once felt like a private miracle became a message I knew I had to share. Not for recognition, not for answers, but for those who have walked through pain and wondered if it meant anything at all. If there's one thing I want people to take from my story, it's that heaven is real and that even in pain, there is purpose. Every soul finds its way home, and every event, no matter how strange or tragic, fits within a pattern of love. Grace is never far away. You just have to believe.

CHAPTER 5
TWO WORLDS UNDER ONE ROOF

Years passed after the shooting, and childhood, with its persistence, slowly carried me forward. I went to school, tried to make friends, and learned to live quietly with the things I saw but could never explain. They became part of me like silent companions I couldn't name, yet couldn't forget. I learned to smile when I was supposed to, to nod along when others spoke of ordinary things, and to keep my stories tucked away where no one could reach them. On the outside, I looked like any ordinary girl. On the inside, I was always straddling two worlds, the earthly one everyone else lived in, and the unseen one that never let me go.

As I grew older, the divide between those worlds didn't disappear; it deepened. I became adept at navigating both, though never fully belonging to either. By the time I became a woman, I longed for a life that was simple, predictable, and safe. I didn't want miracles, messages, or shadows in the night. I wanted mornings with coffee, a home filled with laughter, and a life that made sense. For a while, I believed I had found that with Bob.

We built a life, moved through our days like any other family, and settled into a rhythm that looked, at least from the outside, beautifully normal. But even as I folded myself into marriage and motherhood, I always knew the unseen had not released me. It lingered softly, like breath on the back of my neck, and quietly, like a whisper in a still room. I was learning to live in two worlds, and sooner or later, both would make themselves known.

In the beginning, our life was ordinary in the most comforting way. I always woke first. The house would still be half-asleep, quiet except for the kitchen clock and the gurgle of the coffeepot. I'd pack Michael's daycare things, rub sleep from my eyes, and start the day. By the time Bob drifted into the kitchen, his hair flattened, voice low and groggy, I'd already have his mug ready.

"Coffee?" I'd ask.

"Yeah, Kath. Make it strong," he'd mumble, the same way every morning.

After dropping Michael off, we'd drive to work together. Same road, same radio, same life. It wasn't glamorous, but it was dependable, and for a girl who had lived her whole childhood seeing things no one else could, dependability was its own kind of heaven. There was a peace in knowing what came next, in the predictability of traffic lights and weather reports.

Bob was a good provider, a steady man. He didn't speak in grand gestures or poetic declarations, but in actions. He took care of the house so I could work and go to school at night to give us a better future. We made a simple deal: *I'll earn more. You run the home.* And he did, without complaint. He cooked. He cleaned. He washed. He picked up Michael. He folded the laundry. He fed the dogs. So if love could be measured in chores, Bob loved me plenty.

Of course, no life is without its friction. There were habits of his I hated, like smoking. He had smoked since he was a little boy, unbelievably young, and by the time we met, it was as much a part of him as his quiet demeanor. Still, I couldn't stand it in the house.

"Outside," I'd say, and he'd oblige, stepping out onto the porch without protest. He never argued, never made it a point of contention. He respected my dislike for it, but I still didn't like it. Eventually, he quit. Not because I demanded it, but because he knew it was killing him. That was Bob: emotionally distant, yet deeply responsible. He didn't always say what he felt, but he showed it in the choices he made. It was a small thing, but it showed how much we had to work through, how we each had to give a little.

We had to work through a lot, and we did. We learned to bend without breaking, to give without keeping score. He wasn't the kind of man who held your face in his hands and told you he couldn't live without you. But he was the kind who remembered to buy your favorite tea when you were sick, who fixed the leaky faucet before you even noticed it was dripping, who made sure the car was warm before you stepped outside on a cold morning. His love was practical, almost invisible, but it was there, woven into our everyday life.

Emotionally, though, we were different in almost every way. He was a storm contained in silence. Serious, guarded, carrying old wounds he never spoke of. He held everything in. I didn't. That alone made us opposites. My feelings lived at the surface, always ready to spill over; his stayed locked behind his ribs, guarded like secrets. My patience came from my father. His quick temper came from his blood, Italian heat that rose fast and loud, then burned out just as quickly. When he snapped, I went quiet. When anger filled the room, I stepped outside, walked the block, and let the air unclench us both. That was our dance: his fire, my retreat, and the silence that followed was like a truce.

Still, we had tenderness. We had rituals. We watched TV at night, shoulders touching, saying little but sharing everything. We took

Michael to Myrtle Beach or Florida on family trips, where the sun softened us and laughter came with ease. On weekends, Bob golfed. I sat outside with the sun on my skin and a Stephen King novel in my hands, porch, pool, anywhere I could breathe. I never liked being closed in. The yard, the sky, the air, those were my places. Even now, something in me pulls toward Savannah, Georgia, as if I lived there once in another lifetime. I've never been, but I feel it in my bones, like a memory that doesn't belong to this life.

On paper, our life was steady. Predictable and safe. But paper is thin, and underneath it, the other world waited. It always had.

The first break in normalcy came quietly. A heaviness in the air. A sense of being watched. A shift in a room that shouldn't have shifted. I didn't say anything at first. Bob didn't understand my world, and I didn't want fear to get ahead of the truth. So I kept it to myself, tucked it away like a secret in a drawer. We pretended everything was fine, because pretending is the only thing that keeps the world from falling apart.

Sometimes, in the early hours, I'd wake for water, and the dogs would follow. Our two German shepherds were sensitive to things I couldn't always explain. Every so often, they'd freeze halfway down the hall, muscles tense, ears up, eyes locked on the kitchen sink. A low growl would rise from their throats, deep and instinctive. I'd feel it too, that quiet pressure in the room, like something unseen had stepped in.

"I know you're here," I said softly, not startled, just aware.

The dogs would growl a little longer, then settle. Whatever it was would leave, and I'd go back to bed. It didn't happen every night, but often enough that it became part of the rhythm, like a creak of the stairs or the hum of the fridge. The dogs' growls deepened, vibrating through the floor became another sound in the house's quiet symphony. I never feared it, not exactly. I just knew it was part of the landscape I'd always lived with.

And so, life went on in daylight. We went to church when we could. We sat in silence when words were too small. And when I became pregnant, Bob grew more protective. He watched me more closely, locked the doors earlier, and drove slower. I blessed the crib, hung a crucifix, and prayed over our home. For a little while, peace returned, sweet and gentle, like God pressed His palm against our roof to cover us through those months.

After Michael was born, the house softened. Bob, without hesitation, took on the mothering role while I worked long hours and on-call nights. He fed Michael, folded tiny clothes, paced floors with a baby on his shoulder. It bonded us in a way that no vow or promise ever could. Parenthood does that; it ties a knot that arguments can't easily cut. In those early years, I held my child and felt heaven closer than it had ever been. Creation opens a window to the Creator, and through that window, I glimpsed something holy.

But peace, like all things, proved temporary. As Michael grew, the shadows stirred again. Not all at once, but gradually, like dust gathering in corners. One presence in particular refused to leave. It darted through rooms, hid in corners, and fed tension into the walls. I saw it plain as day once, small, dark, with a single horn on its forehead, the size of a small dog. It ran through the house as if it owned it. TV screens flickered. Closets felt crowded. Our moods shifted for no earthly reason. Even Bob began to feel it.

"I saw it," he whispered one night, eyes still fixed on the TV. "Kath, it just ran across the screen."

That was the day disbelief died in him.

From then on, something shifted in Bob. He hated feeling powerless. Bob is a man who fixes what is broken. He's the one who tightens loose screws, patches holes, and replaces what's worn. But you can't swing a hammer at the unseen. So he did the only thing he could: he fought it the way he knew how. He would stand in the center of a room and shout into the air, "Get out of here! Do you hear me? Get out!" His fear translated as anger. His helplessness came out as a fight. And in a way, that too was love, standing up to something he couldn't see, for me.

We tried everything we could think of. At one point, we even let a TV crew into our home once. Meters, cameras, experts with calm voices and curious eyes. They walked through our rooms, asked their questions, and set up their equipment. But they left with nothing. No readings, no proof, nothing. And we stayed with everything. The spirits didn't hide. They didn't flicker lights or chill the air like in stories people tell when they don't know what they're dealing with. They moved plainly through the house. I saw them as clearly as I saw the furniture. They passed through doorways, lingered in corners, and sometimes watched from the edges of rooms. Not every spirit was malicious, but none belonged.

It wasn't a surprise anymore. It was routine. I'd be folding laundry, and one would drift past the doorway. I'd be brushing my teeth, and feel eyes behind me in the mirror. I didn't scream. I didn't run. I simply lived with it, the way some people live with chronic pain or a memory that won't fade. You learn to keep moving.

But every so often, one would step forward, bold, intrusive, claiming space it had no right to. That's when I stood my ground.

One afternoon, I was carrying an armful of fresh towels. I stepped inside, expecting nothing more than the scent of detergent and the warmth of the dryer. Instead, there it stood—dark, tall, and unmistakably there. Not a shadow. A presence. It pressed against the wall and spoke one word:

"Death."

I didn't run.

"Wait a minute. Not me," I said. "You better not be talking about me. Talk about my cat."

My voice did not tremble. I spoke with the authority God had given me long before I ever knew its purpose. The presence recoiled. Not gone, but stripped of its claim. It lingered, but it no longer held power.

Around that same time, Michael began to see and hear things too. He was young, and it terrified him. I recognized the signs, the way his eyes darted toward corners, the way he clung to me at night. I told him the truth that day, gently but clearly: "You can tell God you don't want this gift." With childlike faith, he asked to be spared. And just like that, it left. It never returned. I thanked God for sparing him my burden.

The house remained a place of thin veils. Some nights, Bob would pause in the hallway, sniff the air, and say, "Do you smell cigarettes?" I never did. But his father had been a heavy smoker. "Maybe he's visiting," I told Bob. It comforted him to think so. In a home where so much was unexplainable, that small idea gave him peace.

Years passed. We fought, we forgave, we worked, we endured. Bob was ten years older than me, and as his body aged, I grew more nurturing. We cared for each other in the quiet, unglamorous ways that matter more than flowers or poetry. Our marriage was not built on grand gestures; it was built on staying.

And through it all, I learned this: you can share a home with someone and battle a world they will never see. You can fight darkness at night and make coffee in the morning. You can stand on holy ground one chapter of your life and in a kitchen the next. You can love a man of earth while serving a God of heaven.

Whenever life felt too heavy, we drove to the water. Bob golfed. I breathed in salt and horizon. Later, he'd sit beside me, our silence softer by the sea. If the drum was chaos, the ocean was my cure. It reminded me that stillness was possible, even when the world inside our walls felt anything but still.

Even now, when I look back, I hear two sounds from those years: the noise of battles I never asked for, and the steady hush of waves that washed me whole.

Peace, I've come to understand, is not the absence of darkness. It's knowing who you are when darkness enters the room. It's choosing faith over fear, again and again. It's blessing a crib, walking through an unseen storm, and believing, without proof, that God will meet you in every shadow.

I didn't just survive those years.

I learned to stand in them.

And soon, I would learn something even harder: awareness is not just seeing. It is discerning, listening, and refusing to bow. The next lesson of my life wasn't new at all. It was a return to what had been with me since childhood, a quiet knowing waiting to be remembered.

CHAPTER 6
LEARNING NOT TO
FEAR WHAT I CAN SEE

Awareness began early for me, earlier than most memories I can trace. I was five when I first realized that what I sensed wasn't just happening *to* me. It was something I could shape and guide. At that age, most children are just beginning to name their feelings, but I was already learning to navigate something invisible. I remember thinking, even then, "Oh boy, this is real." The air felt thicker, the world a little too awake.

From the beginning, I wasn't alone in it. God placed a teacher beside me, a woman in spirit who never scolded or frightened me. She spoke through calm itself. Her peace filled the room before she said anything at all, like sunlight warming a space before it is seen. Sometimes the quiet would roll in first, and my whole body knew—she's here. I'd freeze, half afraid, half relieved.

When fear would crawl up my throat, tight and sudden like a shadow trying to speak, her presence slowed it. No lectures, no noise—just that hush that pressed against my fear until it backed off. I didn't know her name, but I knew her presence. It felt familiar, like something I had known before I was born. It was as if she whispered without sound, *"Don't react. Just stand."*

So I stood. I wanted to run, sure, but something stronger kept my feet down.

Each time the air thickened or the room changed weight, I learned not to scream or flinch. I held still long enough for truth to show itself. That became my first real discipline. It wasn't courage then; it was instinct. If I moved too soon, I knew I'd lose control. I discovered that when you stand quietly, what's false can't pretend for long. Silence has a way of revealing things. She taught me early on: *fear widens doors, but calm closes them.* And once closed, those doors do more than keep danger out. They keep clarity in. You can choose how to respond, instead of being pulled into reaction. It sounds simple now, but back then, it was survival.

That stillness became a habit before I even knew it was strength. It seeped into everything, how I spoke, how I listened, how I waited.

Even as a child, I practiced this until it became second nature. I could be frightened, but never frantic. I could look, but not react. And somehow, that calm changed the space around me. Sometimes I swear the room took a breath when I did. The energy would shift, and what felt threatening would lose its grip. I didn't understand how it worked, but I saw the results again and again.

As I grew, silence became my way of understanding the world. I could sit in a crowd, smiling, nodding, while carrying on another whole conversation in my mind… with the unseen. You'd never know by looking at me. I could be chatting about the weather and, in the same breath, telling a spirit to hush. No one ever noticed. That double awareness, half here, half there, shaped how I moved through life. It wasn't always easy. At first, it felt confusing, like trying to listen to two things at once. Some days I'd walk away from a conversation exhausted, not from people, but from everything else I was hearing beneath them. But over time, the quiet stopped feeling empty. It became my teacher. It taught me patience the hard way by making me sit through every fear until it softened. It taught me to listen before deciding, to sense before responding, and to measure what was real before trusting what appeared.

With that awareness came another lesson: every spirit carried its own kind of energy. Some felt soft and lost, wandering like children who forgot where home was. Some felt restless and bright, curious but harmless. Others were heavy as stone. You could *feel* them before you saw them. A lost soul might not even remember its own name. A lingering one might just want to find its family. When I showed them the light above, sometimes by thinking about it, and sometimes by speaking about it, they rose through it like air finally freed of weight. Those moments filled the room with peace so pure it made everything feel still and safe.

These moments didn't just happen in quiet places. They weren't limited to candlelit rooms or silent nights. Sometimes I'd be brushing my teeth or walking to school, and suddenly the air would shift. It was subtle, like a change in temperature or a sound just out of range. I learned to recognize those moments, not as interruptions, but as invitations. They were calls for attention, not panic. Sometimes they needed help. Sometimes they just needed to be seen. I didn't always have answers, but I had attention. And that was often enough. Presence, I learned, was its own kind of offering.

But not all presences were gentle. Darkness came different—dense, close, and choking, like the air forgot how to move. My chest would tighten, my breath shorten, my skin prickle with warning. That was my signal. My body has always spoken first; it's a quiet alarm built by God Himself. The second that pressure hit my lungs, I knew: something bad's here.

And I learned early that fear belongs to evil, but awareness belongs to God. So instead of running, I stood taller. I'd straighten my back, lift my chin, and make myself *feel* ten feet high. "You cannot have me," I'd say inside. Sometimes I whispered it out loud, teeth clenched, just to hear the sound of strength. Every time I did, the dark lost power. It can't feed where peace stands still. That truth became my shield.

As the years passed, I began to understand the uniqueness of each spirit. Every spirit had its own "fingerprint." Some arrived like storms, sudden and overwhelming. Others came like songs half-remembered, soft and fragmented, carrying pieces of who they used to be. Each one brushed against me with its own unfinished story, a kind of emotional residue that lingered in the air. I learned to meet them with calm, not confrontation. If I stayed steady, they quieted; if I wavered, they fed off it. Their nearness could stir my pulse, but I never let their energy become mine. That separation was essential. If one got too loud or fast, I'd tell it quietly, *Calm down.* And they always did. Stillness carries authority that shouting never will, and they know it. It's not about the volume but the certainty.

That understanding was tested one night in a way I'll never forget. It was late, and the house was too quiet. I was half-asleep on the couch when the air in my living room snapped awake. A man appeared, pacing back and forth, his outline solid one moment and flickering the next. He wasn't mist or shadow; he looked real, like a man who had walked in from the street and lost his way. His boots struck the floor without sound, but I could feel every step inside my chest. He was restless, desperate, muttering over and over that he shouldn't be dead. His voice wasn't coming through the air; it was inside my mind, sharp and fast, too fast. Every word made my pulse match his rhythm until my heart felt like it was trying to escape my ribs. I remember pressing my hand against it, whispering, "Slow down, that's not yours."

I didn't scream. I didn't even stand up. I wanted to, God knows I wanted to, but the training was stronger than the panic. I stared right at him and said, "Who are you?" My voice came out lower than I expected, like it had borrowed courage from somewhere holy. Then I asked for a sign. In an instant, a picture flashed in my mind: someone I knew from work. His children were about to find out what had happened. He wanted me to call their mother. In that moment, I felt the weight of his urgency. It pressed on my skin like heat, made the walls feel closer. For a moment, I couldn't tell where he ended, and I began. That's how strong he came through. But I also knew my limits. That panic wasn't mine to carry. I wasn't meant to deliver every message or fix every story. When he pressed too close, I lifted my hand and said, "Back off."

And he did. Just like that, he stopped. It was like a switch flipped, the room's pressure broke, the air cooled, and suddenly I could breathe again. I sat there shaking, every muscle vibrating with leftover fear, whispering, "Thank You," over and over.

When it was over, I just sat there for a long while, letting the silence rebuild itself around me. Calm had spoken louder than fear, and I finally understood what that meant. That's how boundaries work in the spirit world. They aren't built from words but from faith. I never needed elaborate prayers or special rituals. A clear intention, steady belief, and one firm command were enough. Because they needed help, they listened. True authority doesn't come from force. It listens first, speaks once, and everything around it obeys.

As I grew more experienced, my awareness shifted. It became less about seeing and more about *managing myself while I saw.* The real work was internal. Breathing, posture, stillness—these became my armor. When the energy around me spun fast, I slowed within. I learned to anchor myself. Sometimes I'd literally step back, take a breath, and remind myself: *they can't harm you.* Even when proof of harm came, I held my ground. But the first time it happened, I'll be honest, I was terrified. I woke up one morning and my arms were on fire. Scratches crossed my skin in long, red tracks, angry and raised, like something had tried to write on me in pain.

They burned so bad I gasped out loud. I remember sitting up fast, the sheets twisted, my heart slamming against my chest. For a second, I thought I was bleeding. The marks pulsed, hot and stinging, as if the darkness had left fingerprints behind.

They didn't want to be acknowledged, and my awareness threatened their hiding place. The first time, I cried, yes. I'm not ashamed of that. The pain wasn't just physical; it was disbelief, anger, and defiance all at once. But when the shaking passed, I did what I'd been taught since I was five: I stood. I prayed, slow and steady, until the fear thinned out of the air. I remembered what my teacher had said—*fear feeds what it focuses on.* They could touch flesh, not faith. The marks faded. The strength stayed. I learned that pain doesn't always mean danger; it can also mean resistance to light. And light, when held firmly, always wins.

After that, I promised myself I'd never wait until the fear turned to pain again. When the air shifted, I'd call on God sooner. I learned to invite peace before panic even had the chance to breathe.

When things grew too heavy, I called on God or Archangel Michael, and they came instantly, not as visions, but as a shift in the air. Warmth would fill the room, pressure would ease, and peace would return. It was subtle but unmistakable, like the feeling of someone standing beside you even when you can't see them. Once, when grief hollowed me so deeply that I couldn't speak, I felt hands on each side of my face, lifting my chin toward light. That's how angels speak, not through words, but through presence. In that warmth, my sadness melted. Not all at once, but enough to breathe again.

After that, my prayers changed. They stopped sounding like *please help me* and started sounding like *thank you for helping.* I realized God hears the whisper before it even forms. I didn't need to explain or plead. I just needed to trust. That shift in understanding changed everything. It rewrote the way I saw my gift. I stopped seeing my gift as a haunting and began seeing it as an assignment. God had chosen me to help guide the lost, to lift the wandering, to send light where fear once lived. I've watched souls rise into light, relieved, weightless, home. And it was then I stopped asking *Why me?* And started saying *Use me.* That shift, from questioning to offering, marked the beginning of true service.

Awareness became service, not survival. It wasn't about fighting darkness anymore. It was about carrying peace. I didn't need to battle what was broken. I needed to hold what was whole. I didn't need to swing swords at shadows; I just had to stand still long enough for light to fill the room. That clarity gave me direction. It taught me that peace isn't passive, it's powerful.

From that service, certain truths wrote themselves into my life. They didn't come from books or teachings. They came from experience, from moments that tested me and shaped me. The first truth I learned was that fear feeds what it focuses on. The more I gave attention to fear, the more it grew, drawing strength from my uncertainty. But when I shifted my focus to peace, fear lost its grip.

That led me to the next realization: authority doesn't come from force, but from certainty. When I stood firm in what I knew, without hesitation or apology, spirits responded. They didn't need to be shouted at. They needed to feel that I meant what I said. From there, I began to see how curiosity, though often harmless in the physical world, could be risky in the spiritual one. It opens doors that peace would rather keep closed. I had to learn that not every presence should be engaged, and not every question needs an answer. Discernment became just as important as compassion. Knowing when to help and when to step back was part of the work.

And silence, when grounded in faith, governs the room. It doesn't just quiet the noise; it sets the tone. It creates a boundary without walls, a presence without force. That kind of silence speaks louder than words, and it carries a strength that spirits recognize immediately.

These weren't lessons I found in books or learned from others. They weren't memorized or recited. They came from living. They taught me when to speak and when to stay still, because not every spirit should be answered. I learned to wait for God's nudge—the gentle *this one needs you* or *let this one pass.* Some spirits just walk the echoes of their old lives, and peace means letting them be.

As I grew older, my guide no longer walked beside me, but her lessons deepened inside me. Her presence faded, but her wisdom remained. Intuition became like breathing. I could feel a room before entering, sense danger before the door even opened, and know when not to step forward. My body itself became an instrument of discernment; the gooseflesh, the tight lungs, the sudden warmth that told me holiness was near. Sometimes it was just a flutter under my ribs or a weight behind my eyes. Those were God's quiet signals. I no longer resisted them; I thanked Him for them, even when they came without explanation.

There were days I felt weary, wishing the veil would close just long enough for me to rest. I longed for a moment where the world felt simple again, where I could move without sensing, speak without filtering, sleep without waking to whispers. But peace always returned, the way breath returns after running. God never left me in the dark for long. I learned that awareness wasn't about what I encountered; it was about who I became in each encounter. I didn't have to prove my strength to darkness. I only had to remain steady until it left. And it always did. Not because I was powerful, but because I was anchored.

Looking back, I see that God had been shaping me all along, not to survive two worlds, but to walk between them without fear. He wasn't training me to endure. He was teaching me to carry. Awareness became the quiet armor of that calling. It was simple, unseen, and strong. Through awareness, I found discipline. Through silence, I discovered strength. Through fear, I learned faith. And through faith, I found peace that didn't depend on circumstance.

Now I move through both worlds with the same calm that woman once taught me, knowing that what stands before me must bow to the One who stands within me.

The world still holds shadows, but I don't fear them anymore. I carry light, and light is louder than fear. I am no longer a witness to the unseen. I am a warrior shaped by it. Every encounter, every silence, every moment of stillness has formed something strong in me. And awareness is the armor that never leaves me.

CHAPTER 7
PROTECTING MY PEACE
ABOVE ALL ELSE

There comes a stage in life when a gift settles into you. It stops feeling like something that surprises you or frightens you. It no longer feels foreign or unpredictable. Instead, it becomes something you move with, something you understand in a way that only time and experience can teach. You stop wondering why it chose you. One day, you notice that the fear has softened, that the questions have quieted, and that the gift no longer feels like something outside of you. It has become yours. When I look back at the girl I was, the one who flinched at every shift in the room and lived in a constant state of anticipation, I feel a deep tenderness. She was doing her best with what she had. She was learning to navigate a world that often felt too loud, too sharp, too uncertain. But even then, she was growing. And now, standing where I am, I can see how far she has come.

I no longer live in fear. I no longer brace before turning a corner, expecting something to leap out and undo me. The years have given me something steadier. I have become calmer, more grounded in myself, and far more certain of how to meet whatever comes. That certainty is not arrogance. It is trust. Trust in the path I have walked, in the strength I have built, and in the quiet knowing that I have already survived so much.

Nothing about the gift feels heavy anymore. I live with it the same way someone lives with their own breath. I do not feel weighed down.

I simply move with it, and when something approaches, I take it as it comes. That is what maturity does. It teaches you to trust what years of experience have already proven: that you will handle it, and that you will not be hurt. I live my life normally, go about my days, and if someone from the other side steps forward, I deal with it and continue on. It is peaceful in its own way.

When I think back to what Jesus said to me when I was two years old, that He was sending me back with a gift, at the time, I could not possibly understand the weight of those words. I was a child, barely beginning to form memories, let alone make sense of them. But now, with the perspective of adulthood, I see it differently. I see it not just as a moment of divine intervention, but as a calling. It was a responsibility; a decision made for reasons far greater than I understood at the time. I was chosen, and not everybody is. That is something I never take lightly. I feel fortunate, honored even, because He gave it to me knowing I could handle it. I cherish the gift now. I do not question it, I do not try to return it, and I do not resent it. It was given to me because I was strong enough to carry it.

The shift from simple awareness to actually *living* with the gift came later, not in childhood when so much was already frightening and confusing, but as I grew into adulthood. After high school, when life becomes something you start thinking about instead of simply surviving, and when the world begins to ask you who you are and what you believe, I found myself looking at everything I had been through. It was then that I understood just how much responsibility I had been carrying all along. I realized I was chosen for a reason, and that something like this is never placed on someone who cannot bear it.

My life back then felt unsettled, full of nerves and constant uncertainty. Every experience felt sharp, unpredictable, and overwhelming. I was a nervous child, easily startled, unsure of what was coming next. The world felt too big, too loud, and I often found myself shrinking from it, trying to stay small enough not to be noticed. I lived in a state of quiet anticipation, always bracing for something I couldn't name. Now everything is different. I am steady. I do not get rattled. I move through my days with calmness, and the gift enhances my life instead of interrupting it. I feel fortunate, even blessed, to live with something that allows me to help others, even when they are no longer living. That kind of connection is rare, and I do not take it for granted.

There are moments that remind me why the gift matters, moments that stop you long enough to recognize the purpose behind it all. One of those moments came through a spirit who was lost, unable to find the light on their own. "I can't find it... I don't see the light," he whispered, his voice trembling with fear. He looked more afraid than I ever was, and in that moment, I felt the weight of what I had been given. When I helped them cross and heard the rush of his departure, I felt that deep, warm feeling wash over me, and I understood again what this gift was meant to do. There is nothing like helping someone find their way home. It is rewarding in a way that fills you from the inside, like a spiritual warmth that lingers long after they are gone. That feeling is impossible to describe unless you've lived it—an overwhelming, almost church-like warmth, the kind of peace that moves through every part of you when they finally go where they belong.

And sometimes, that responsibility comes in unexpected forms. Years ago, a small boy from the 1800s found his way to me. He was no more than four, his voice so small I had to bend down to hear him. "I'm lost," he told me once, standing at the edge of my bedroom doorway. "I don't know where to go." He followed me everywhere — to work, in the car, even sleeping beside me because he felt safe. One night, I knelt beside him and said, "Look up... that light is for you. Your parents are waiting." His face softened with relief. And in a breath, a warm, rushing swoosh, he was gone. Helping him go home was one of the first times I truly understood what it meant to live with this gift rather than simply endure it. It was no longer something that happened to me. It was something I could use to bring peace.

Living with this gift also taught me something else: who belongs in my life and who does not. I know instantly. Sometimes all I need to do is take one step toward someone, and my whole body says, "No... not this one." At other times, without thinking, something in me relaxes, and I know, "This person is good." The body knows long before the mind catches up. Some people carry heaviness or secrets that press against me the moment they get close. Others feel light, warm, and good the second they enter the room. My senses make the choice long before my mind gets involved.

That sensitivity has shaped the way I choose my circle. Some people have energy that complements mine, and others do not. I do not invite negativity, drama, or chaos into my world. My circle has stayed small for that reason. And when someone doesn't belong, I don't confront, argue, or announce it. And when someone isn't meant for me, I don't argue or explain. I simply feel myself stepping back, inch by inch, until one day I realize there is distance and peace again. "Let it fade," I tell myself. "Your peace matters more."

That circle is made up of people who have earned their place beside me. Dottie has been with me for as long as I can remember, and she knows more about my life than anyone. She listens, supports, and understands without needing explanations. She has walked through good times and painful times with me, and she never questions my experiences. In the mornings, when the phone rings at six, she'll say, "Okay, tell me everything." And I do, because with her, I never have to protect or shrink any part of myself. She listens the way only someone who truly loves you can—quietly, without judgment, without trying to fix anything. Because sometimes listening is the greatest gift a person can offer. And with her, I am always safe.

That kind of safety is rare, but I've been fortunate to find it more than once. Sue is another one who understands on a deep level, because she has abilities of her own, even if they appear differently. She has been in my life for many years; someone I can sit with quietly when life gets heavy. There were times when we didn't need to speak at all. I would simply sit beside her through her struggles, offering presence instead of words. Some friendships don't need noise. They just need space, and they grow on their own like dandelions.

Stephanie is also part of that circle in her own way, kind and steady, with energy that does not disturb or weigh down. Her presence is gentle, and her support never feels forced. These women have shown me that the right people do not need to be taught how to treat you; they simply do it.

Because of that, letting people go has always been easier for me than holding onto something that does not feel right. I do not make a scene or engage in confrontations. I simply step back until the distance becomes natural. At times, I think about people who once held a larger place in my life, wondering how they are doing, but I do not feel regret when someone fades out. If anything, I feel lighter, physically lighter, because holding onto the wrong people always feels like carrying weight that was never mine. And if someone reappears after years, I am kind and polite, but I do not reopen the space they once had. My peace matters too much to risk it out of obligation. I have learned that not every connection is meant to last forever, and that honoring my own peace is not selfish; it is necessary.

This gift has also taught me that peace is something you feel in your body long before you understand it in your mind. I can always tell when something disturbs the balance around me. Spirits who need to manifest will drain energy as naturally as breathing, and I recognize the shift immediately. When someone from the living brings chaos instead of calm, I feel that too. It is not always loud or obvious. Sometimes it is just a subtle tension, a quiet disruption in the air. I protect my peace by keeping my home quiet, maintaining simple routines, and making my mornings slow. I wake early, sit with my coffee, watch the news, and ease into the day before the world stirs. My house may not always be peaceful in every corner, but I carve out the spaces I need. I create moments of stillness, places where I can breathe without interruption. That is how I stay grounded.

Some of the most peaceful moments I have lately are in the backyard with my dogs. I step outside, and they watch me with excitement, waiting for the ball. "Ready?" I ask them, even though they always are. I throw it across the yard, and they dart after it with a joy that makes everything in me settle. The yard is open and quiet. They run, they return, they drop the ball at my feet, tongues out, eyes bright, as if they know they are returning me to myself. In those moments, I feel grounded, connected to something simple and good. It reminds me that peace can come from the smallest things. Out there, I often tell myself, "This is enough. Right here, this is peace."

That same clarity extends to the people in my life. I do not test people through long conversations or drawn-out interactions. One step toward them tells me all I need to know. If the energy feels off, I don't let them get any closer. I do not ask God who to keep or who to release. He gave me the senses and discernment to know that myself. I pray when I truly need help, when something darker tries to interfere. But for everyday decisions about people, I rely on what I have learned. Discernment is quiet. It lives in the body. And with age, I have learned to trust that quiet instinct more than anything spoken out loud.

That trust in myself has been hard-earned. Looking back at who I used to be and who I am now, I can see how different those two versions of me are. I used to be scared, unaware of my own strength, unsure of what the next moment would bring. I lived in a state of constant anticipation, always waiting for something to go wrong. Now I stand tall in what I know. I trust myself. I trust my instincts. I understand now that spirits see a golden glow around me—something I never knew growing up. They recognize it as a safe haven, a place of purity, and a refuge where they can come for help. Learning that changed everything. It helped me understand why they come and why they trust me. That realization brought not only clarity, but also compassion—for them, and for the younger version of myself who once felt so overwhelmed by their presence.

If I could speak to my younger self, I would tell her that she will always be protected. I would tell her not to waste time being afraid, because help is never far. I would tell her she is stronger than she can imagine, and that her gift is nothing to fear. I would tell her that boundaries are not selfish, that peace is worth protecting, and that solitude does not mean she is alone. I would tell her that quiet strength is still strength, and that the people meant for her will never make her feel heavy.

And if someone reading this finds themselves in that same space of uncertainty, I hope they take this with them: peace is something you create. It is not something you wait for or stumble into. You choose who enters your life. You choose who stays. You choose what kind of energy you allow around you. Everyone has a sense inside them, even if they do not have a gift like mine. Everyone has that moment when they turn suddenly because something inside them tells them someone is there. That sense is real. That awareness is part of being human.

My gift has taught me that not everything that comes toward you is meant to stay. Discernment is just as important as bravery. Peace is just as important as strength. And the small circle you keep close can be more powerful than a crowd of people who never understood you to begin with.

I live with the gift now in a way that feels natural, steady, and purposeful. It no longer shakes me. It guides me, and I let it. I no longer resist its presence or question its timing. I move with it, and in doing so, I move with peace.

CHAPTER 8
WHAT THE LIGHT
TEACHES IN THE DARK

There are moments in this work when the only thing I can do, the only thing that actually matters, is to be completely still. Not the kind of stillness that people mistake for hesitation or passivity, but the kind that hums with awareness. People think that being a medium is all about performing, saying the right thing, offering comfort, and announcing some big message from the other side. They picture spirits lined up like actors waiting for their cue, eager for their spotlight.

But the truth, the real truth that took me years to learn, is that the work starts long before a single word is spoken. It starts in silence. And silence, when you know how to listen, is never empty. It is charged, alive, like the air itself is holding its breath, waiting for something unseen to arrive.

That is why stillness became my greatest teacher. It showed me what no class, no mentor, no textbook ever could. Stillness is not absence; it is presence sharpened to a fine edge. It is respect for what is already here but not yet revealed. It is attention so complete that even the smallest shift in energy feels like thunder. And sometimes, stillness is survival.

From that understanding came a habit, a discipline: listening before acting. There have been so many times when something inside me said, *Don't move. Listen first. Let the room speak before you do.* And that inner voice has never been wrong. Each time I obeyed it, I discovered that silence had already prepared the ground for what was about to unfold.

One of the clearest lessons in that came during a night that, to anyone else, would have seemed utterly ordinary. I was simply at work, doing my job as an ultrasound tech down in the hospital basement. Nobody thinks about that part of the building. At night, it feels like the whole world forgets it exists. The machines sleep, the hallways echo differently, the lights hum that low, steady tone, and the stillness wraps around you like a glass dome.

And in that stillness, even the smallest details mattered. My desk faced the wall, which meant the door was always behind me. Most people hate sitting like that. They want to see who's coming, to keep their back safe. Me? I got used to it. That night, around eight o'clock, the quiet felt heavier than usual. Not scary. Not threatening. Just... full. Like something was in the room with me, but hadn't made itself known yet.

Now, this is where people expect me to say I jumped up, spun around, screamed, something dramatic. Nope. That's not how it happened. I stayed seated. Hands folded in my lap. Back straight. Breath steady. I didn't force my eyes to search. I let my senses do the work.

Because in my world, feeling always comes first. Seeing comes second.

And when I finally turned, there they were.

Two men standing in the doorway—not mist, not shadows, not something you could brush off as imagination. Solid. Present. Native American. Dressed in full regalia, like they stepped right out of their time and into mine. One was a chief, feathers trailing down his back in a long sweep that made me straighten my posture instantly, like I'd just entered the presence of royalty. His war paint wasn't decorative. It carried meaning, weight, and intention. I couldn't translate it, but I could feel it, deep in my chest, like a vibration that resonated with something older than language.

Next to him stood a warrior. He held a long stick with an arrow attached, feathers tied near the end, his face marked with strong, deliberate lines of paint. His presence was calm and strong. They were not wandering. They were not confused. They were exactly where they meant to be.

Most people imagine they'd scream or faint at such a sight. They picture panic, a rush of adrenaline, the body betraying the mind. But what rose up in me was recognition, a quiet certainty that this was not intrusion but intention. My chest tightened, not with fear, but with awareness.

Okay, I thought. *They want something.*

So I stayed still.

The chief didn't speak out loud. His lips never moved, yet his voice filled my mind, clear and direct, the way spirits do when they know exactly what they need. There was no mistaking it, no haze of imagination. He told me he needed help. And I remember thinking, almost laughing inside my chest, *What could I possibly do for a chief who lived a whole other lifetime?*

That's when he told me he had seen me at my Thursday night psychic development class.

That stopped me, not in fear, but in shock, like when someone mentions a private detail you didn't expect them to know. That class was something I did to get out of the house, stretch my abilities, and spend time with my friend Sue. Every Thursday, I picked her up, and we went together, chatting in the car, sharing stories, treating it as both practice and ritual. It wasn't anything I expected a chief from another time to know about. The idea that he had been there, watching, unsettled me in a way that was not frightening but deeply humbling.

But he wanted me to take him there.

Not someday.

Tomorrow.

I told him yes. The word came out simple, like dropping a pebble in water. And apparently, that was all he needed.

He followed me home that night. I swear, he sat on my sofa like he had an appointment scheduled, like he was waiting for his name to be called. The TV was on, but I couldn't tell you what show. The ordinary stuff, the lamp, the books on the coffee table, the hum of the fridge, all of it faded. The room felt like it had been repurposed, like my living room was suddenly a waiting room for something bigger. The next day, he rode in the back seat of my car like it was the most normal thing in the world. Maybe to him, it was. He didn't blink at traffic lights, didn't care about honking horns or billboards. He just sat there, steady, like he'd been riding in cars forever.

But here's the thing—I didn't drive straight to class. I went to pick up Sue first. I needed her energy. Her grounding. She's the kind of friend who makes you feel like your feet are on the floor even when your head's in the clouds. The chief didn't like that one bit. You could feel the air tighten, like when someone's mad but hasn't said it yet. Not rage, but definitely disapproval. I explained, in my mind, that Sue was my friend and she was coming. Period. She was my friend, my anchor, and she was part of this. He didn't argue, but the silence that followed was heavy, like he was tolerating it but not thrilled.

When we reached the building, I left Sue in the car and went inside to talk to my instructor. I told her the ground needed to be blessed. Not suggested. Not recommended. Needed. And she looked at me like I had grown a second head. You know that look people give when they're trying to smile but their eyes are saying, *What planet are you from?* That was her. And the thing is, she knew me. She'd seen me read people, seen me stand up in front of the class and deliver messages that landed so hard folks cried. She believed I had a gift. But even with all that, she told me no.

Not because she thought I was making it up. Not because she doubted me. No, because she wanted ghost hunters to come. She wanted the cameras, the drama, the money. She wanted to use the spirits instead of helping them. And that cut me deep.

And the chief... he was one of the reasons that the basement felt the way it did. Sue and I had gone down there before, touched the walls, and felt bodies beneath the ground. You don't forget that. That land carried their story, and it deserved respect.

I told her, firm and clear:

"If you don't bless the ground, this place isn't going to survive."

She refused.

Sue and I left, and I was furious. The kind of fury that makes your chest tight and your words come out before you even think them through. I turned to her and said, "This place isn't going to be here anymore." It wasn't a prediction I wanted to make; it was a truth I could feel pressing against me.

And sure enough, within a year, the building was gone. Just… gone. Torn down, erased, like it had never stood there at all. And when that happened, I finally understood the weight of what I'd felt that night.

The chief taught me something that wouldn't make sense until much later—that stillness wasn't just how I protected myself in strange basements or hospital hallways. It was how I stayed open. It was how I heard what others couldn't. And one day, that silence and that listening wouldn't belong to a stranger at all. It would belong to someone I loved.

Before he died, I told my father something I had never said to anyone in my family. I looked him straight in the eye and said, "When you die, come to me." I didn't say it out of fear or denial. I said it because I knew what I could do. I knew I could help him. Being a medium doesn't stop at the edge of your personal life. One day, the work comes home to you.

And when he passed, he did exactly what I asked. I was driving home from work when suddenly his energy filled the car—solid, familiar, unmistakable. The moment I realized he was gone, the grief hit me so hard that the tears came before the thought did. Losing my dad and having him appear in the same breath was like being split in two. But even through the crying, I didn't panic. I didn't run. I stayed still. I listened. I let him come to me.

Guiding him to the light showed me something that nothing else ever had. This wasn't just a skill I used for strangers who wandered into my space. This was love and duty meeting in the exact same moment, and stillness was the only way I could hold both without breaking. Helping my father cross made the lesson real: calm isn't just control—it's compassion. It's how I honor the living and the dead.

After that moment, I understood something I hadn't fully grasped before: if I could stay present in the most painful crossing of my life, then I could stay present for anyone.

That's when I finally understood the heart of this work: listening isn't passive. Listening is an action. Listening is power. Stillness opens the door, whether it's a stranger in a basement or your own father finding his way home.

Once a spirit trusts me, really trusts me, the whole atmosphere shifts. It's like the world rearranges itself so it's just the two of us tucked into a smaller, quieter space. I never know when it's going to happen. I could be surrounded by people, in the middle of noise, in a room full of movement—and the second a spirit opens up, all of that falls away like someone closed a curtain behind me. It becomes just the two of us, standing inside a kind of tunnel where no one else exists. I don't hear the room anymore. I don't feel the air the same way. I'm not even aware of my own body the way I usually am. I'm fully present, but not present in the world everyone else is standing in. I can see them, but they're not part of the moment.

Sometimes I forget I'm even sitting or standing. I forget if I'm holding something. I don't hear regular sounds, just the feeling of the spirit's energy shaping itself into words. And that "watched" feeling—that's the first sign something is opening. It settles on me like someone put a hand on the back of my shoulder, not touching the skin but touching the air around it. The hairs on my arms stand up, but not from fear; it's more like recognition, like the moment before someone speaks your name.

That's how I know a spirit has opened up.

People always think the first thing I pick up is their story, but no. Their energy arrives before anything else. That's always the introduction. I can tell who was soft in life, who was loud, who was angry, who was ignored, and who never had anyone listen to them. Some come in shy, hovering like they're afraid to bother me. Some burst in like a door flying open, talking a mile a minute. Some arrive frantic, their energy jittering through my whole body. And some drift through the room so quietly it feels like a sigh.

And then there are the ones who don't even notice me. They walk right past with their hands half-raised, like they're frozen mid-gesture, stuck in a moment they can't move out of. Those break my heart. That's confusion, not resistance. They don't know they can talk. They don't know where they are. They're just looping through the last pieces of their life.

But the ones who *do* see me?

They treat me like a lifeline.

They've been walking the earth for so long without anyone hearing them that when they finally find someone who can, they rush in. They don't ease into it. They unload everything at once. Their energy hits like electricity, sharp and desperate for a landing place. And if I don't stay grounded, if I don't slow them down, everything spirals.

That's when I lift my hand and say, in my mind or sometimes out loud,

"Slow down. Bring it down. One thing at a time. I can't help you if you're spinning like that."

And every single time, they settle. The frantic edge softens, the storm quiets, and suddenly we're back in that smaller, quieter space again.

It's like watching a warm current calm into a steady stream; you can feel the shift in your bones.

That's when I realized something huge: Calm is power. Fear gives them control. Calm gives it back to me. If I stay steady, they meet me there. If I let fear in, their energy explodes. Fear is like wind on a flame. Calm smooths it back down into something I can hold, something I can work with.

And here's the thing: people always assume the hardest part is wrangling the frantic ones, the ones who come in like a hurricane. But no. The hardest moments aren't the wild ones; they're the ones where the spirit doesn't trust me yet. That mistrust hangs heavy, like a weight pressing on my chest. The air thickens, almost sticky, and I can feel them hovering close, circling me like they're testing the waters, searching for a reason to believe I'm safe.

And that's when I say gently:

"You have to trust me. If you don't trust me, you're going to be walking forever."

I don't say it like a lecture. I say it like a lifeline, like I'm tossing them a rope across a river. Sometimes I feel that hesitation loosen, little by little, until belief finally clicks into place. And when it does, they go fast, like they've been waiting for permission all along. Sometimes I hear a soft swoosh, like air sliding through a tiny doorway. Sometimes the whole room lightens, as if someone cracked open a window. And sometimes, I feel the softest kiss on my cheek, just a brush of warmth, so delicate it makes me laugh under my breath, like they're saying thank you in the only way they can.

And then they're gone.

Once they leave, the world comes rushing back. I feel my body again. I notice the chair under me, the hum of the refrigerator, and the sound of traffic outside. I take a breath—the kind that reminds me I'm here, alive, grounded. And I always smile after. Not a big grin, just enough to feel it tug at my face. Because I know I did something good. I helped someone get home. And that's no small thing.

But not all spirits come gentle. And this is where people's Hollywood ideas about the afterlife crash into reality. Some spirits come angry, arrogant, cruel—exactly how they were when they were alive. Death doesn't cleanse a soul. Personality stays. If they were mean here, they're mean there. And I don't let that near me.

I put up a wall. A shield I picture rising right in front of me—solid, heavy, unmoving. I don't whisper it, I don't ask politely. I say it with absolute conviction: "No. You don't come near me." Because here's the truth: you can't whisper boundaries in this work. You state them, and you mean them. And they feel that. Spirits know when you're bluffing. They know when you're shaky. And if you're shaky, they'll push.

Some test it. I've had one come at me with enough anger that if he'd had physical hands, he would've grabbed my throat. And let me tell you, that's not the kind of moment you prepare for in psychic development class. Nobody hands you a manual for "what to do when a furious spirit tries to choke you." But I didn't flinch. I raised that shield higher. If they want help crossing, I'll help them. But they follow *my* rules. Always.

Respect doesn't end with death. That lesson changed everything for me, because boundaries with spirits taught me boundaries with people. Funny how that works—you think you're learning how to deal with the unseen, but really, you're learning how to deal with the living too. I can feel someone's energy the moment they walk into my life. Some people feel soft, warm, right. Others make something inside me tighten, like a warning bell ringing low in my chest. And I listen to that now. If I don't allow chaos from the dead, I'm sure as hell not allowing it from the living.

Peace is not something I negotiate. My protection isn't about big rituals. It's steady habits that anchor me. I shower with salt or use salt-based soaps and lotions from spiritual shops. Salt scrapes off energy that tries to cling. I've lined my house with it before—sometimes it helps, sometimes a determined spirit finds a way anyway.

I wear my crucifix because I'm Catholic. I keep crosses on my nightstand and around the house. But honestly? More than any object, it's my confidence and my faith that protect me. The shield starts in me, not around me.

People always ask how I stay safe doing this work, and the answer is the same as every lesson I've learned: Stay calm. Stay present. Stay firm. Don't feed fear. Don't run. Don't let anything, spirit or person, step past the line where your peace lives.

And I've tested those rules in every kind of space. I've walked through cold rooms that made my skin prickle, heavy rooms where the air felt broken, rooms where silence pressed so hard it felt like sound itself had been stolen. I've seen shadows slip across walls, chiefs standing tall in full regalia, warriors with paint marking their faces, and lost souls who were just looking for someone, anyone, to hear them.

Through all of it, one truth has followed me from that hospital basement to every place a spirit has found me: I am stronger when I listen first. Stillness is my foundation. Confidence is my armor. And the light I carry is bigger than anything that steps into my space.

CHAPTER 9
BREAKING THE SILENCE
FOR THOSE LIKE ME

If someone had told me years ago that I would one day sit down and share all of this, every part of my journey, every experience with my gift, every truth I kept hidden from almost everyone, I would've laughed. Not because I thought it was impossible, but because talking about myself like this has never been easy. I'm the kind of person who handles things quietly, processes things privately, and keeps my personal life tight and protected. My circle is small for a reason. Opening up goes against how I've lived most of my life.

Silence always felt safer than explaining myself. When you grow up and live with something spiritual, something heavy, and something you can't always explain to others, silence becomes a kind of protection. I learned to live that way. I learned to act like everything around me was normal, even when what I was experiencing was anything but.

So people might think there was some big, dramatic moment that made me finally open up. Some huge event that pushed me into writing this down. But it really wasn't like that. It wasn't a sudden shock or a single thing that changed everything. It happened slowly. It was built over time. Memories surfaced at unexpected moments and reminded me of the parts of my life I had carried alone for so long. It came from little moments that kept repeating themselves: memories coming back unexpectedly, feelings pushing forward, thoughts that wouldn't leave me alone. It felt almost like God was tapping me on the shoulder every now and then, gently reminding me, "You can't keep this inside forever."

As these memories returned, I started to feel the weight of carrying everything alone. I began to notice how heavy silence had become and how long I had walked through life believing I was the only one feeling these things. Those quiet reminders slowly pushed me toward the truth that I couldn't keep everything inside forever. It wasn't a single moment; it was years of small reminders. And eventually, after enough of them, you reach a point where you can't ignore it anymore. You start to feel like your story isn't just something you lived, it's something that might help someone else. You start to realize that maybe your silence has stopped serving you.

And that's exactly what happened to me.

I never wanted attention. I wasn't looking for sympathy or approval or validation. I wasn't trying to prove anything. But I did start thinking about the people out there who might have similar experiences, who might have gifts like mine, who might be struggling in silence, confused or afraid. And that made me think about how alone I felt for so many years. I didn't have anyone to talk to except my brother Walt, and even then, it wasn't like I unloaded everything on him. Most of the time, I just kept it to myself because explaining it felt too complicated. My friends didn't know. My coworkers didn't know. Even people who had known me for years had no idea what I carried.

But over time, silence turns into pressure. It becomes this weight that sits in your chest and never fully goes away. That's what started happening to me as I got older. I didn't even realize it at first. I would just feel tired, emotionally tired, without understanding why.

Eventually, it hit me. Staying quiet was draining me. It was taking a toll I didn't want to admit. I was holding everything in, every experience, every moment, every thing I never explained, and it sat on my shoulders like a huge invisible weight. And it made me think: *Why am I still carrying this alone? Why am I still pretending this part of my life doesn't exist?*

That's when I started considering the idea of opening up. Not because I suddenly felt brave or ready, but because I realized my silence wasn't protecting me anymore. It was actually making things heavier. Opening up became less about courage and more about allowing myself to breathe again.

I also realized something important:

There are people out there who need to hear stories like this.

Not because they're looking for entertainment. Not because they want something spooky to read. But because they're living their own silent battles. Some have gifts they don't understand. Some are dealing with spiritual encounters they're scared to mention to anyone. Some feel emotions and energies that don't belong to them and have no idea how to explain them. Some went through trauma and think they're the only ones who came out of it with spiritual sensitivity.

Those are the people I thought about the most. The ones sitting quietly at home, thinking something is wrong with them, thinking no one else in the world is experiencing what they experience. Those are the people who made me say, *Maybe it's time to talk. Maybe if I open my mouth, someone out there will finally feel seen.*

And so, slowly, I started to accept the idea of opening up. Not all at once. But piece by piece. Every small step made the next one a little easier.

One of the biggest things that held me back for so long was fear, real fear, of people not believing me. That fear ran deeper than anything spiritual I ever dealt with. I wasn't scared of the spirits. I wasn't scared of the things I saw. I wasn't scared of the dark moments or the strange moments or the moments that didn't make sense. I had been dealing with those things all my life. What scared me was the thought of telling people who've known me for years and hearing them say, "No… that can't be true."

So many people around me have known me for decades, but they only knew the parts of me I allowed them to see. They knew the friendly parts, the strong parts, the quiet parts, the hardworking parts, but they never saw the spiritual side of my life. They never knew about the things I've been dealing with since childhood. They never knew the depth of what I've survived.

Some of the closest people in my life had absolutely no idea what my inner world looked like, and the thought of revealing it was overwhelming. No one else in my immediate family knew, not my other siblings, not my father while he was living, not even some of my closest friends who have sat at my kitchen table a hundred times. We could talk about life, kids, work, relationships, everything, but not this.

So when I started thinking about sharing my story publicly, that fear came right back. *What will they think when they read this? How will they react? Will they believe me?* I didn't want people thinking I was making things up. I didn't want to become the topic of whispers or judgments. I didn't want to be doubted.

That fear stayed with me for a long time. And even now, as I write this, there's still a small part of me that feels nervous about how people will take it. But something in me changed. I reached a point where I realized that holding back my truth to avoid someone else's disbelief wasn't fair to me. I also realized that people who truly know me, the ones who actually see my character, would understand that I'd never lie about something like this. And if someone chooses not to believe me, then that's their choice. I can't live my life based on what someone else might think.

The truth is, the fear of not being believed was only part of what kept me quiet. Another part was the responsibility that comes with having a gift. When you experience things spiritually, when you see and feel things others can't, you carry a responsibility that doesn't always have instructions. You just deal with it the best way you can. And for me, silence was my way of dealing with it. I didn't know how to explain what I went through, and I didn't want people misunderstanding something that was such a big part of my life.

But after thinking about it deeply, I realized something important:

Maybe the very thing I was afraid to talk about was the thing someone else needed to hear.

There are people out there right now who have gifts they don't understand. People who wake up feeling energy that isn't theirs. People who sense things in their homes. People who see figures in the corner of their eye and brush it off. People who feel heaviness in rooms before they step inside. People who feel like they're going crazy because they can't explain what they're experiencing.

Those people aren't crazy. They're not imagining things. They're not alone. They're dealing with something real. I know because I lived it, too. And for years, I had no one to say that to me. I didn't have a book like this to pick up. I didn't have a story like mine to compare my life to. I had to figure it out on my own. And that's why opening up became important to me. Because someone out there might pick up this book and finally understand themselves.

I want people with similar gifts to read this and feel comfort instead of fear. I want them to see that yes, it's challenging; yes, it can be overwhelming; yes, it can feel isolating, but it's also survivable. It doesn't have to break you. If anything, it can make you stronger.

And for the people who feel alone, I want them to know they're not alone. Even if they don't talk about what they experience. Even if they don't tell their spouse, their friends, or their family, there are others who live through these things every day. People like me. People like them. They might not talk about it, but they exist. Many people choose silence because it feels safer, and I understand that—but even in that silence, they are not alone.

I also want to be clear:

You don't have to talk about your experiences if you're not ready.

This is something I feel strongly about. Just because I'm choosing to open up now doesn't mean everyone else needs to. Speaking up is a personal choice, not a requirement. If someone has a gift and they want to keep it private, that's completely fine. If someone feels scared to talk, that's fine too. I didn't talk for years, not because I was ashamed, but because I didn't know how, and I wasn't ready.

So when I think about other mediums, sensitives, or spiritual people who are terrified to speak up, I want to give them permission—not to talk, but to take their time. They can read. They can learn. They can grow privately. They can build boundaries and protect themselves. They don't have to speak until *they* feel ready. If they never feel ready, that's fine too. Not everyone is meant to share publicly. Some people live their whole lives quietly, and they're still doing exactly what they're meant to do.

Talking about my experiences hasn't made me weaker or more vulnerable. It's done the exact opposite. It's made me feel stronger, more grounded, more sure of who I am. And that's something I didn't expect when I first decided to speak.

One of the biggest changes that happened to me once I started talking about my gift was the shift in how I saw myself. When you keep something hidden for most of your life, you start to view it as something that needs to stay in the dark. Not because it's bad, but because silence becomes your comfort zone. You get used to staying quiet. You get used to protecting yourself by not saying too much. And after years of doing that, you begin to think of your own experiences as something that shouldn't be shared.

But opening up changed that for me. For the first time, I began to see myself without the filter of silence. It made me see myself differently, not as someone who had to hide, but as someone who could finally breathe a little easier. I realized I had been carrying these huge pieces of my life in silence, and letting them out made me feel lighter. I felt stronger, more confident, and more sure of my own abilities.

It didn't turn me into a different person, but it did make me more grounded. I started looking at my life and thinking, *I went through all of that. I survived that. And now I'm strong enough to talk about it.*

I'm spiritually stronger, emotionally stronger, and mentally stronger. I've always been strong, but speaking about these things made me recognize it in a way I never did before.

Another thing that changed was the way I approach other people's energy. Once you start talking about your gift, more people come to you with questions or stories or emotions they want to unload. People get curious. People want advice. People want to share their own experiences with you. And that can be overwhelming if you don't protect your energy.

I've learned to do that naturally. I've always done it privately, but now it's even more important since talking about my gift invites more energy from others. I protect myself by building a mental wall. I don't let everyone's emotions into my space. People carry their own struggles, fears, and energies—some heavy, some chaotic, some confusing. And if you're sensitive, you can feel that immediately when someone steps close to you.

When someone approaches me too quickly or too intensely, I feel that spiritual "electricity" from their energy. It hits me before they even open their mouth. And I've learned to give myself space. I literally step back, put one foot behind the other to get distance, because I can't let myself get caught in someone else's chaos. Once they calm down, once their energy settles, that's when I can talk to them. But protecting my boundaries is something I take seriously.

Spiritual people, mediums, or anyone with a gift needs boundaries. Without them, you drain yourself without even realizing it. Now that I'm opening up, I protect my energy in a different way: by separating myself from anything that feels too heavy, too intense, or too chaotic.

When I think back on the years when I had no one to talk to, I remember how I relied on any bit of understanding I could find. Books, quiet research, and the stories of others became the only places where I could see pieces of my own experiences reflected back at me. Those moments of learning helped me make sense of what I was living through. They gave me something solid to hold onto when everything felt confusing.

All of that shaped the way I see my gift now. Every bit of knowledge I gathered over time helped me stand where I am today, more grounded and more certain of myself than I ever was before.

And through all of this, I've come to understand something important about survival. I've been through trauma more than once. Big trauma, small trauma, all kinds. And each time, I didn't fall apart. I didn't stay broken. I became stronger, not in a dramatic way, but in a real, everyday-life kind of way. Trauma changes you, but surviving it builds you. Every time you go through something difficult and come out the other side, you become a stronger version of yourself.

A lot of people think trauma is something that should weaken you, but I don't believe that. Trauma tests you, but it also builds you. You learn to say, "I can do this." You learn to say, "I've been through worse." You grow resilience without even realizing it. That's what happened to me, and that's what I hope other survivors take away from this chapter. Not pity—strength.

I've also learned the importance of knowledge: reading, researching, and educating yourself. I've spent countless hours in libraries and bookstores, Barnes & Noble being my favorite, because learning helps you make sense of your own gift. Books by others who lived through similar things gave me comfort when I had no one else to talk to. Those pages became companions during the years when I was carrying everything alone.

As I close this chapter, I think about how long it took me to get here—years of silence, years of fear, years of carrying everything alone. And now, writing all of this, I realize I'm finally allowing myself to be seen for who I truly am. I'm not hiding anymore. I'm not pretending. I'm not minimizing what I've been through. I'm putting it on paper honestly, clearly, and in my own voice.

I'm opening up because it's time.

Because I'm ready. Because I've survived too much to stay quiet any longer. Because someone out there needs to know they're not alone. Because my silence was heavy, and sharing is lighter.

This chapter is my truth. This chapter is the doorway I'm finally walking through after a lifetime of keeping it closed. And I hope, more than anything, that it helps someone finally start to understand themselves.

CHAPTER 10
THE WOMAN
DARKNESS CANNOT SILENCE

There comes a time in your life when you finally understand yourself in a clear, steady way. You don't need someone to explain your past, and you don't second-guess your instincts the way you once did. Everything you lived through starts to make sense, not because someone else confirmed it, but because you've been living with that truth for so long that it has settled into who you are. It feels less like discovery and more like recognition—like meeting yourself again after years of carrying fragments you didn't know how to piece together. I've reached that point. It didn't happen overnight. It happened slowly, through experience, through silence, and through every moment when I had to rely on my own awareness to get through things nobody else even noticed. And when I look back now, I realize that every time I stood alone, every time I trusted my own perception, I was building a foundation that could hold me steady no matter what came next.

When I think about my childhood, I can see the difference between other kids and me more clearly than ever. Kids react to everything, they scream when something startles them, they run to adults when something feels strange, they ask a thousand questions because that's how they learn. I didn't do any of that. I didn't scream. I didn't point. I didn't ask. Instead, I learned early to keep my reactions hidden, to stay quiet, to look away when something wanted me to look directly at it. Where most children had the freedom to be surprised or curious, I had responsibility. I had awareness. I had training that forced me to grow up differently. And while they were learning through play, I was learning through vigilance, through the discipline of noticing what others missed and carrying it silently.

Even now, as an adult, that early training hasn't left me. My instincts are stronger than ever. My body reacts before anything else: tightness in my chest, a shift in the air, a sense that something is trying to move closer than it should. And my shepherds feel it too. They're calm dogs until something is wrong. Then they stiffen, they stare, they growl, and it's enough to let me know I'm not imagining anything. Their reactions line up with my instincts, and that lets me stay grounded instead of getting thrown off balance. It's a partnership built on trust; my awareness and their presence reinforcing each other, reminding me that steadiness is not isolation but connection.

I've learned that the first sign of negative energy isn't fear—it's being drained for no reason. Out of nowhere, I'll feel wiped out, or irritated, or heavy. That's when I sit quietly and ask myself, "Is this mine?" Ninety percent of the time, it's not. Once I separate what belongs to me from what doesn't, the pressure lifts. That's something nobody teaches you. It's something you learn by going through it again and again until the pattern becomes clear. And once you see it, you begin to trust yourself more deeply—you stop doubting your own perception, because you've proven it to yourself too many times to ignore.

People have a lot of assumptions about strength. They think it has to be loud or aggressive, but that's not how I operate. My strength is steady. It's in my tone, my posture, my decision not to react. It's in not letting anything dark see weakness on my face. I don't have to fight or yell. My stillness is enough. Negative energy doesn't like someone who doesn't flinch. It wants someone who shakes, someone who doubts. It doesn't get that from me anymore. And the more I practice this, the more I realize that strength isn't about overpowering; it's about refusing to be moved by what doesn't deserve your movement.

My peace today looks completely different from the peace I had when I was young. Back then, peace meant getting through the day without something happening. Now, peace means knowing that whatever does happen, I can handle it. And because I carry that calm, I've become more aware of what unsettles it. Crowds, for example, drain me. They feel like noise in a way most people don't understand, a constant pull on my energy that leaves me hollow. I prefer fewer people, quieter spaces, and energy that doesn't overwhelm me. My shepherds stay close because they protect me in their own way. They've got instincts just as sharp as mine, and together we keep things steady.

When something tries to push against my peace, I know exactly how to take control. Sometimes that means putting salt around the home to set boundaries, a physical reminder that my space is mine. Sometimes it means picturing myself standing taller and stronger than anything trying to approach me. And when something really tries to cross a line, I call on Archangel Michael. He has never hesitated to protect me. His presence is immediate, unwavering, and it reminds me that I am never alone in this. The presence of God in my life is something I don't need to talk about every day, but I feel it. It's steady. It's immediate. And it's stronger than anything that tries to test me. That strength is not loud, but absolute.

People with gifts often feel isolated because they don't have guidance. I've met enough people to know how lost they can feel, wandering through experiences they don't understand. And I genuinely feel bad for them, not in a judgmental way, but because I know what it's like to face something with no one explaining it. Confusion can feel heavier than the gift itself. If I could, I would teach people what I've learned. Not theories. Not dramatic stories. Real steps. Real clarity. Real boundaries. Nobody should have to figure this out alone, stumbling through trial and error when wisdom could be shared.

At this point in my life, I understand myself in a way that leaves no room for confusion. I never lost myself because I was quiet. If anything, silence helped me find who I was. It forced me to develop strength in places other people overlook. It helped me recognize my own authority, the kind that doesn't need validation. My gift didn't weaken me; it shaped me into someone who doesn't break easily. And now, I move through my life with a calmness that comes from knowing I'm protected, guided, and fully aware of what's around me.

I don't see myself as someone darkness can push around anymore. I don't live in fear. I don't even hesitate. I know when something is near, I know how to handle it, and I know it cannot cross the boundary I set. Negative energy reacts to me because it knows I see it, and it knows I'm not affected by it the way I once was. There's no advantage to be gained from someone who stands their ground every time. And when you stand long enough, darkness learns to keep its distance. It recognizes strength when it meets it, and strength that doesn't waver becomes a wall it cannot climb.

And for anyone reading this who feels targeted, overwhelmed, or misunderstood because of their gift, I want you to hear this clearly:

You're not crazy. You're not imagining things. You're not weak. You just need to trust yourself more than you trust your fear. Fear will always try to speak louder, but your awareness is sharper than fear if you let it be. If something drains you, pay attention. If something feels wrong, don't ignore it. You don't have to give everything a reaction— just a recognition. And if you ever feel alone in your experiences, remember that many people with gifts have lived through similar things. You're not the only one, even if it feels that way. Isolation is a trick darkness plays, but connection exists—even if it's quiet, even if it's unseen.

If I could sit down with people who have gifts but no guidance, I would teach them the basics of holding their space and protecting their energy. I'd tell them not to panic, not to fold, and not to assume weakness just because they're sensitive. Sensitivity isn't weakness. It's clarity. It's awareness. It's the ability to notice what others miss. And once you learn how to control it, it becomes one of the strongest things you'll ever carry. Sensitivity sharpens instinct, and instinct sharpens survival. It's not about being fragile—it's about being tuned in. And when you're tuned in, you can stand steady in places where others stumble.

When I look at my life now, I can see the difference between the person I was and the woman I've become. I'm not unsure anymore. I'm not afraid of what comes around me. I don't hesitate when something tries to get close. I handle it. I move on. And I don't let it shape my day or my mood. That kind of power comes from experience, not ego. It comes from knowing yourself inside and out, from walking through storms and realizing you didn't break. It comes from silence that taught me patience, from solitude that taught me strength, and from faith that taught me resilience.

And that's why negative energy reacts to me the way it does now. Not because I chase it. Not because I want to fight it. Not because I think I'm bigger than anything. But because I don't bend—not emotionally, not spiritually, not mentally. I've learned that bending to fear only feeds it, while standing firm starves it. After everything I've seen, everything I've lived, and everything I've learned to control, I can say this with complete confidence:

Negative energy doesn't threaten me.

I threaten it.

Not by force.

But by standing firm in who I am, every single time.

www.ingramcontent.com/pod-product-compliance
Lightning Source LLC
Chambersburg PA
CBHW051233120626
46547CB00013B/1628